A Light To India

A Light To India

Lillian Doerksen

with Dan Wooding

WinePress Publishing
MUKILTEO, WA 98275

Printed in the United States of America

Packaged by WinePress Publishing, PO Box 1406, Mukilteo, WA 98275. The views expressed or implied in this work do not necessarily reflect those of WinePress Publishing. Ultimate design, content, and editorial accuracy of this work is the responsibility of the author(s).

Cover: Love and Radiant Joy Beams from the Hearts and Lives of the Precious Deaf Touched by the Beams of the Light of the World.

ISBN 1-57921-075-9
Library of Congress Catalog Card Number: 97-62216

CONTENTS

Acknowledgments iii
Foreword v

Chapter One
   A Big Decision 11
Chapter Two
   In The Beginning . . . God 21
Chapter Three
   All Change 33
Chapter Four
   Please Sanctify My Smeller 45
Chapter Five
   The Place of the Palms 55
Chapter Six
   Honeysuckle Wonders 71
Chapter Seven
   The Wagon of Light 93

Chapter Eight
  Preparing for Leadership 107
Chapter Nine
  Don't Wrestle, Just Nestle 117
Chapter Ten
  The Prayer Tower 133
Chapter Eleven
  A Message for the Dalai Lama 147
Chapter Twelve
  An Imperfect Sacrifice 157
Chapter Thirteen
  My Second Call 173
Chapter Fourteen
  Rock of Ages 189
Chapter Fifteen
  The Deaf Shall Hear 203
Chapter Sixteen
  In Aurangabad, Too 209
Chapter Seventeen
  India's Cornerstones 221

Epilogue 225
About the Authors 231

ACKNOWLEDGMENTS

I would like to place on record my heartfelt thanks to Dan Wooding for helping me put this book together. Having been born on the mission field—in Nigeria—of British missionary parents, and having also visited India, he was able to help me capture my story in this book.

I would also like to thank his wife, Norma, who took forty-six years of my writings and put them in files so that I could access them more easily when we started writing the book.

Of course, I deeply appreciate the kind and wonderful hospitality of George and Cindy Payton, who made their home in Chino Hills, California, available for Dan and me to work on the book. George is, of course, the president of our US board of the Maharashtra Fellowship of Deaf (MFD).

Deep thanks are also in order to Ted and Audrey Beckett of Colorado Springs, Colorado, for introducing me to Dan Wooding and also for generously helping to provide the resources for the writing to take place.

I also wish to thank my Canadian and US boards of the MFD for their unflagging support of the mission God has called me to in India and also for the staff there who are doing such a magnificent job in being *a light to India*.

FOREWORD

When we think of India, it is easy to be overwhelmed by the sheer magnitude of the physical suffering and poverty there; to become so discouraged by the enormity of the problems that it seems impossible to even try to meet any of the urgent needs. But the Lord doesn't ask us to do it all—just to be faithful in the tasks He has assigned to us.

Although these thoughts and feelings probably went through Lillian's mind when the Lord called her to India as a young woman, she responded positively to that call, and "left all and followed Him." Once the decision was made, she never looked back.

The years that followed proved to be challenging, fulfilling and not without hardship, as Lillian used her teaching, organizational and mothering skills. She was never satisfied with the status quo but constantly looked for ways to improve the lives of the Mukti girls. Always energetic and enthusiastic, Lillian suggested innovations in curriculum, methods and living arrangements, and dared to stand by her convictions.

Lillian and I became friends in our twenties as we attended the Metropolitan Tabernacle in Vancouver, B.C. Although our paths led us to different parts of North America and beyond we kept in touch over the years. When the company I worked for transferred me back to Vancouver, Lillian and the Canadian Council of the RMM asked me to assume the executive secretary position, which I held for ten years. During those years, I visited the Pandita Ramabai Mukti Mission three times. Upon my return to the US, I took over a similar position for the Maharashtra Fellowship for Deaf. In 1991, I spent four months in Pune with Lillian and the directors. During those visits I had ample opportunity to observe her work and witness first hand some of the fruits of her faithful and untiring labors.

This book is not merely another biography but the inspirational story of a woman who dedicated a lifetime to the spiritual and physical welfare of the girls and women of Mukti, and the deaf young people of Maharashtra, in a country she loved. Should the reading of this book result in others giving their lives to bring the good news and hope of the gospel to India, it would be one of Lillian's greatest joys.

Lillian would want all the glory to go to her Lord, but with the writer of Proverbs we can acknowledge: "It is the God-fearing woman who is honoured. Extol her for the fruit of all her toil, and let her labours bring her honour" (New English Bible).

VIOLA DAND
Pacific Northwest Regional Director
SERVE

Chapter One

A Big Decision

The receptionist peered over her eyeglasses and smiled as she handed me the telegram. "This has just arrived for you," she said as I walked into the lobby from the street after working my afternoon job at a local department store. "I hope it's good news!"

Standing in the foyer of the Bible Institute of Los Angeles (BIOLA) in downtown Los Angeles, which had a huge JESUS SAVES sign by the building, I ripped open the envelope. With shaking hands and racing heartbeat, I read the words: "EMBARKATION LEAVE. STOP. COMING FRIDAY TO DECIDE DATE OF WEDDING. STOP. LOVE, LLOYD. STOP."

Lloyd James was a handsome six-footer who was in the Royal Canadian Air Force. Thick color began to rise in my cheeks as I stared at it thunderstruck. His telegram was not good news for me at that moment, for he was planning to make the trip from Vancouver in British Columbia to see me. I guess I should have been excited, but instead I felt a wave of anxiety wash over me, as I knew that he would not

In Front of the Big "Jesus Saves" Sign, Downtown BIOLA Building

understand what I was going to have to tell him. There was no way now, however, to contact him to ask him to wait for a more appropriate time.

To add to my dilemma, I had agreed to spend the weekend at a ski lodge in the spectacular redwoods with a group of students from BIOLA, founded in 1908, where I was attending.

To pay for my tuition fees, I had taken a job at the nearby huge Robinson's department store. So, the following day, I was not able to catch the college bus that was transporting the rest of the students to the ski lodge in northern California. The president of BIOLA, who was leaving later for the college camp, had heard of my predicament. He was to be the main speaker at this retreat and suggested I drive up there with him, as he would be leaving after I got off work. That next afternoon as I tried to concentrate on my duties in the foreign woolens' department at the store, I found my thoughts slipping back to when Lloyd and I had first met. It had been two years previous—1945—and I had been helping as a volunteer at the Soldiers, Sailors and Airman's Christian Association in Vancouver, BC. The war in Europe was grinding to a halt after those terrible five years of bloodshed and carnage. My countrymen from Canada had joined with the Allies in pushing back Adolph Hitler and his storm troopers to his bunker in Berlin.

Many young people like me had joined the war effort by helping out at Christian servicemen's clubs like this one. I was twenty-six years old and had gone out with other boyfriends, but none had been long-standing relationships. The day I met Lloyd wearing his blue "flyer" uniform at the club, he immediately began talking to me and our friendship began. When he later asked me out, I agreed, and so began some lovely times together in a nearby restaurant. It was then that I discovered that he was, like me, a Christian. Soon Lloyd was attending church with me and also joining me for our young people's outings. Our relationship blossomed quickly. During his days off from the air force, we would go out for day trips to see the sights of Vancouver. We especially enjoyed mountain climbing. He would go out to my home in Abbotsford, not far away, and my family grew fond of him, too.

"Lil," he said one day, holding my hand as we walked up the snow-covered Grouse Mountain that towered above the city, "do you think you would be happy living in Toronto?"

"Why do you ask?" I responded, wondering where this question was leading.

"Well," he said, pausing for a long moment, "you see, that's where I am from and I was thinking that maybe we could spend our lives together."

I was stunned. Trying to get a grip on my whirling thoughts, I finally pulled myself together and responded. "Lloyd," I began in a soft voice, "that would be great, but I would have to be very sure that it was God's will."

Lloyd was obviously disappointed. I am sure he was hoping that I would give him a more positive answer.

"Please let me pray about it," I continued, "then I'll let you know what the Lord shows me."

Just a short time after this, Lloyd, who had not seen service overseas, was posted for a whole year to the Northwest Territories of northern Canada. So began a new relationship via the mail. We became pen pals. Lloyd knew my family and the young people at my church, and consequently we would write about all that was going on in our lives. His letters were always a delight to read, and I knew that he loved me. I was beginning to be more attracted to him.

While Lloyd was "up north," I began to feel the need to complete Bible training with the possible view of becoming a missionary to a land far away. I had already had two years in the Briercrest Bible Institute in Saskatchewan and had a wonderful time there being trained in God's Word. I could not go back to graduate because of a decision that my father had made.

A friend of mine was attending the Bible Institute of Los Angeles. She was able to get me admitted there for more classes and also a job in the afternoons at Robinson's department store, just one block away. So, to complete my training, I moved to Los Angeles—The City of Angels— and really began to enjoy my studies there.

Regularly, I would pray and ask God to show me what He wanted for my life and where He wanted me to serve. It was not long before a series of incidents began to occur that would also cause me to think again about my future with Lloyd.

Initially, I had thought that maybe I could serve the Lord in Toronto or possibly Lloyd would be willing to become a missionary, too.

It was now 1947 and the war in Europe and the Pacific had ended. Many missionaries who had not been able to return home for furlough began appearing in the States. Some came to speak to us at our chapel service at BIOLA.

Previously, I did not remember ever hearing a missionary from India, but now there seemed to be one after another coming to our institute. They would powerfully lay out the need for the gospel to be preached in India, a vast land with the world's second largest population. These missionaries talked about the teeming millions in that far-away land who knew nothing of Christ, as the majority of the people there were Hindus. All I could think about now was India. The country and need there were becoming imbedded in my heart.

A Challenge On the Way to Tinsel Town

Each student at BIOLA was given a practical work assignment. Mine was to be the leader of the junior church at the Calvary Church of Hollywood. Being brought up in rural Canada, the name Hollywood had such a glamorous ring to it, and I was excited to be actually able to visit it. I was assigned to travel with Carol Terry, an enthusiastic woman who had been called as a missionary to India. I soon discovered that this church had been supporting her.

Each Sunday, Carol and I would catch the tram from downtown Los Angeles to Hollywood. She would use that travel time to tell me about the mission she had been assigned to.

But first Carol told me about her traumatic experiences during the war. "Lil," she said one day as the tram hummed along the tracks toward the movie capital, "I had been accepted as a missionary with the Pandita Ramabai Mukti Mission and was on a ship from Los Angeles to Bombay when the Japanese captured our ship. We were all taken prisoner and kept in terrible conditions in a camp in Manila, Philippines.

"We were treated very cruelly and not given enough food to eat. As the war in the Pacific was coming to an end, the Japanese decided to execute all of us by shooting us. Just two days before we were to be killed, American paratroopers came into the camp and rescued us. It was a great miracle! God spared our lives and I was sent back to the States to recover."

I was stunned to hear Carol's story and also amazed at the lack of bitterness in her voice as she said, "I am still hoping to go back and work for the Pandita Ramabai Mukti Mission."

Carol could see that I was speechless about her wartime experience and so went on to explain a little more about this mission. "*Mukti*," she said, "means salvation. They have over 800 orphans in their care and so much need our help. That's why I am going back. They have babies, children, orphans, widows, the blind or handicapped, and each one of them go through their care and are helped.

"Pandita Ramabai was an Indian woman who, before the turn of the century, was a reformer and a wonderful 'mother' to thousands of starving, destitute girls, child widows, and young women whom she rescued, took into her Home of Salvation, loved and educated."

Carol added that Pandita Ramabai founded this home in 1868 in Kedgoan, in the state of Maharashtra.

That night when I got back to my quarters, I found that I could not sleep. The image of all those children left without hope gave me such sorrow. (Carol, by the way, years later, married Dr. Louis Talbot, who became the president of BIOLA University and has a school of theology—Talbot School of Theology—named after him.)

Night after night, I would toss and turn, contemplating the children of India. I also found myself beginning to protest to God. As I knelt by the side of my bed late one evening, I told the Lord, "God, I don't know if I could cope with the heat, the sickness and the wild animals of India. But if You really want me to go there, please make me able to cope with all of these things."

Carol Terry never gave up on me. She just kept telling me all of the stories of the mission that she was going to work for. She had done deputation work and had slides, books and literature, and she made sure that I had all of them. When Carol saw that I was becoming hooked, she invited the secretary of the US council from Philadelphia to come and interview me. I became very burdened for this work in India, but when I learned that there were no men on the staff, I began to lose interest. I suppose I had a sneaking suspicion that Lloyd might not want to go to India with me. I hoped that maybe there would be a husband at the mission for me!

I had always had fine boyfriends and was sure that I was meant to be married. I was corresponding with Lloyd, whom I loved dearly, and who was looking forward to marrying me when he got out of the air force. I prayed that maybe he would become interested in missionary work and that perhaps we could go to India together.

Exams and graduation time was looming near, and I found it difficult to concentrate. A battle was raging in my heart. I now had a deep concern for the orphan children in India who needed the love of Christ, but I also really desired to get married. I was anguished about how this would all work out. Carol had put me on the mailing list of her mission to receive the monthly literature from Mukti. It contained a leaflet called *Buds and Blossoms,* and in each issue there was a success story of one of those precious children who had been rescued. These captured my attention and burned the need to help them in my heart. Was this God's call of love to my heart?

The BIOLA president who asked me to drive with him to the ski lodge had come down to the lobby and spotted Lloyd sitting quietly in a corner, waiting for me to return from my job. The receptionist had already told Lloyd that I was at work and that I was going to travel with the professor at 5:00 P.M. The president was impressed with the fine looking Canadian airman and told the receptionist, "Oh, he can come with me, too."

With Lloyd at the Ski Lodge Retreat in the Redwoods

When I arrived in the lobby on that Friday afternoon, Lloyd stood up and came over to me and gave me a warm hug. "It's so wonderful to see you again, Lil," he said. "I do hope you are well."

"I'm fine," I spluttered. "Yes, I'm fine."

Soon we set out for the redwoods. The car was huge and we sat together in the front seat with the president at the wheel. His eyes twinkled mischievously as he put romantic music on the car radio. Lloyd reached for my hand. I smiled at him, and we relaxed and communicated silently.

We had a wonderful weekend with all of the students, but I just could not bring myself to tell him of my struggles and God's challenges to my heart. When we returned to Los Angeles on Sunday night, Lloyd told me that he had heard there was a lovely park—Echo Park—nearby, and he would like to take me boating that next evening on the lake there.

"I have to leave on the following morning, and there are some very important decisions to be made," he said as we parted.

As I was about to go to my quarters and Lloyd to the place where he was staying, I told him that it was impossible, as this would be Monday evening and dates were only allowed on weekends. He suggested that I ask the dean anyway, as we had "important decisions" to be discussed. To my surprise, the dean said, "You mean that tall Canadian airman I saw in the lobby? Yes, of course, you may go, but be in by 10:00 p.m." She revealed that she had a brother in Canada and this gave her a soft spot for Canadians.

That Monday evening Lloyd rented a rowboat. After guiding us to the center of the lake, he put down the oars and we just floated along in the moonlight with my head in his lap. Then, out of the blue, looking questioningly at me, he asked, "Lil, why is it that every time I mention anything about the date of our wedding, you change the subject? Even last night when we phoned my mom in Toronto you immediately changed the subject."

"I'm sorry, Lloyd," I said falteringly, acutely conscious of the tension and uncertainty that my actions were causing. "It is not deliberate."

A tear spilled over the bottom curve of one eye and slipped down my cheek. Then I broke down and poured out my heart to him. "Lloyd, I have to be honest with you," I said in a voice that was thick and nervous. "I have been wondering if God wants you to consider the mission field."

There was a long, agonizing silence as he looked at me in mute surprise. His tongue appeared to be locked. Then his face cleared, as did his tongue! "Lil, I have to tell you that I have had no call, nor do I have any inclination to go to the mission field," he said hoarsely. "And besides that, I have my widowed mother to look after." Lloyd took a deep breath and added, "I am sure, Lil, that God is just testing you, like he did Abraham in the Bible. When God saw Abraham was ready to obey Him, he spared his son Isaac's life. I am sure that once God sees you are willing to make this sacrifice, He will give you the assurance that we should get married. He just wants to know that you are willing!"

I shook my head and began to quietly weep. I had hoped that Lloyd would see it my way, but now it did not seem that he would.

Parting that night was so hard for us both. Lloyd said we should both pray and wait for two months to be "very sure" about God's will for both of us.

"Still, I need to know before you graduate in January," he added nervously, stroking his hair.

I smiled neutrally, but said nothing.

Chapter Two

In The Beginning . . . God

The frigid northeast winds swept in off the huge open expanses of the prairies and whistled, howled and moaned down the main street of the tiny town of Herbert, located along Highway 1 in south-central Saskatchewan, Canada. The gusting winds cut through even the thickest clothing like a knife through butter. My mother, Elizabeth Doerksen, a small, but well-built woman, did not notice that the winds were whipping up outside and throwing snow against the window. Lying in bed in a small apartment above the general store where my father worked, she was about to deliver another child—and that was all that mattered to her.

Jacob, my stocky father, who stood about five feet, six inches tall, stoked up the wood-burning stove and waited for the inevitable cry from the baby. At the behest of the

Lillian and Her Family when Her Brother John Returned from Overseas

midwife, my mother continued to "push, push," until I, Lillian Doerksen, finally emerged into this world, crying and very much alive.

The date was March 17, 1921, and I became the second daughter in a family of eight. The oldest was Rosella, then I came next, with Sam, John, Mable, Viola and Orlean, all coming in quick succession, and then Sylvia was born some years later. Another child died at birth, but more about that later.

Fleeing from the Bolsheviks

My father and mother were both Mennonite Brethren of Dutch-German extraction whose parents had settled in the Mennonite village of Osterwick in the Crimean region of Ukraine. The Mennonites, named after Menno Simons

(1496–1561), emerged as part of the era of the sixteenth-century Protestant Reformation in Europe. The Reformation had spawned a number of radical reform groups, among them the Anabaptists. These Christians regarded the Bible as their only rule for faith and life. They denied the merit of infant baptism. Some Anabaptists were revolutionaries. Menno Simons' group were more moderate. Simons, a Dutch priest, gathered the scattered Anabaptists of northern Europe into congregations in 1536. These groups soon came to be called by his name. By the late sixteenth century the Mennonites had found political toleration in the Netherlands. Some groups had moved meanwhile to Poland and to Ukraine, including the families of my grandparents.

But then in 1917, following the Bolshevik Revolution led by Vladimir Lenin, the whole region was under the control of the Bolshevists. Fearing a bloodbath against them because of their German-Dutch background, and also because of their Christian faith, their respective parents fled to the "New World" and settled in north and southcentral Saskatchewan. Both families took up work there. My mother's father had worked in a mill, but when they came to Canada they were given land by the government and became successful farmers. Dad's parents settled in Hepburn, north of Saskatoon.

My father was three at the time and my mother was nine. The emigrants to Canada immediately felt at home, as the area had a similar climate to back home and also because there was already a substantial Mennonite population.

The area began to boom after the railroad was built, but this did not last long. Soon the Great Depression of the 1930s began to bite into the local economy.

It was at a Mennonite Brethren conference that my parents first met and then fell in love and, subsequently, were married.

LIFE IN CANADA

I can still remember my mother preparing Russian borsch, a chicken-beet soup, for us. She would also give us other German-Russian style food, which we all loved.

English was rarely spoken in our house, which did not have electricity. We mainly conversed in what was called Low German—a mixture of German and Dutch—but of course, I soon learned English when I began attending the local primary school.

Eventually, my father had saved enough money to buy his store, which became the second largest in the town. Times were tough during the Depression years. Like his, all of the businesses—such as the blacksmith's and telephone house—all struggled to make ends meet.

Still, we had a happy Christian home. I grew up enjoying regular family prayers, services and Sunday school at the local, white, wooden Mennonite Brethren Church, that had big steps leading up to the entrance. All the proceedings there were conducted in High German, which was the classic German language of that time.

Hanging on a wall in the dining room of our grandparent's home, in a huge frame and inscribed in German in silver, were the words of Psalm 28:2: "For the Lord God is a sun and shield."

We eventually moved to a nearby town, Main Centre, which had sprung up at the end of the railroad line where some huge grain elevators had been built. My father later bought another business that he called Doerksen's General Store. After school hours we all helped there, serving customers from this wheat farming community.

Dad enjoyed taking us out on outings to Lake Peltier and the Saskatchewan River where we had great times swimming and enjoying nature. There were also occasional trips in the truck to Regina when farmers paid Dad what they owed with cows or bulls and he took the animals to Regina to sell them. We were so thrilled when he would take us to horse races and on other interesting excursions. Then there were yearly long family trips to Saskatoon and Hepburn in northern Saskatchewan where his parents and family lived, when we would also visit the exhibition there.

During the long winter months, my father would arrange for a skating rink to be built in our small community of Main Centre, so we could skate and play hockey. We always had our own cow, and I used to enjoy riding her when I had to bring her home. We learned how to milk the cow, and we would save the cream to make ice cream in the little hand freezer.

We always enjoyed visits to our aunts, uncles and cousins. Both Dad and Mother came from large families, but there is now only one aunt left, Aunt Annie Braun, Mother's youngest sister. She takes us all—me and my sisters and brother John and their spouses—out for a grand lunch at least once each time while I am home in Canada. At the time of this writing, she is 87 and still so loving, lots of fun, and deeply involved in what I am doing.

My grandparents, Grandpa and Grandma Nickel, lived a few miles away on a big farm. Our trips there were also fun for us children, with horses to ride and hide and seek to play among the haystacks.

One Sunday afternoon we had to visit friends just a few miles from our home. It was a beautiful summer's day as the sun played tag with a few benign-appearing white clouds. But it all began to change when a man came running towards us in the backyard where we were playing, shouting breathlessly, "Mr. Doerksen, there's smoke coming from the direction of town." We all squinted to see what was on fire. We concluded that it was probably smoke coming from a special train that had come to town.

"Let's head on home," suggested my father. So we forgot about the food that had been laid out. Dad started up his old Model-A Ford and we dashed off. As we got closer, father gasped.

"It's our building that's on fire!" he shouted in anguish. It seemed unbelievable, but as we neared our home it was confirmed that the wooden house that we lived in and the store—that were all one—were now just becoming charred timbers. I watched with eyes that were wide and scared as everything was destroyed.

We later discovered that the fire had been deliberately started by a man who had given my father a fake check, which he was sure was in the store safe. We heard that he confessed that he had ripped the screen off a bedroom window and had thrown in a lighted match.

To add to our troubles, the shock had caused the child that my mother had been carrying to be born dead. We thanked God that mother's life was spared. We held a family funeral for the little mite my parents called Peter Irvin.

After finding temporary accommodation in our grandfather's home, my father was able to purchase the store next door and started to rebuild his business and a house for us.

A TIME OF REBELLION

Like so many teenagers, I began to shy off from partici-
pating in the spiritual activities in our home. I no longer
felt comfortable with the family prayers and was glad for
any excuse to be away. During the long winter months I
loved to go skating and always had a special skating partner. In the short summer there was swimming in the nearby
tank we called a dam, picnics and little outings out of town
to take part in.

Western music had become very popular at that time
and I even learned to yodel. Then Elden, a handsome cowboy from a ranch twelve miles across the Saskatchewan
River, came into my life. He would gallop his strawberry-
roan horse across the bridge into town to secretly date me.
Naturally, I was flattered, but I didn't want my parents to
know what was going on with my first mad crush, as he
was not a Christian.

My parents saw me drifting away from the things they
held dear and were concerned when they realized that I
was choosing entertainment of which they did not approve.
I also took every opportunity to skip our family prayer times.
I knew they were concerned and that they were praying for
me, but I was so carried away with what I thought was
love, I could not resist meeting with Elden.

My little brother John was aware of my romance, and
he agreed to lie for me by making up stories to try to explain my long absences from the house. I became convicted
about what was happening because I knew that my parents
loved me and wanted the best for me. I felt guilty about my
brother, too. I became miserable living this double life.
When my cowboy mentioned that he would like to marry

me if my parents did not want to let me go out with him, I became really frightened. I was only 15 and he was 18. I could not sleep at night and eventually told him that I could not see him anymore. Elden did not give up that easily, and when he came calling, I made one of my girlfriends lie to him and say I wasn't there.

It was a major emotional crisis with my conscience that I could not handle. I found myself saying in the privacy of my bedroom one night, "I wish I could die." I did not want to hurt Elden or my family. I believe that God heard my cry. I began to ask myself, *What if I die? Where would I go?* Surely I was not fit for heaven. It would be hell, and I didn't want to go there. In my distress, God reminded me of John 3:16: "For God so loved the world, that He gave His only begotten Son, that whosoever believeth in Him should not perish, but have everlasting life" (KJV)—which I had learned in Sunday school.

I began to repeat these words out loud. "God so loved the world . . ." But how could He love me? He must know of my sinful heart, my deception and lies. But I was also reminded that God does not lie. I was one of the "world" that He said He loved. That verse said that He gave his only begotten Son, and I seemed to see Jesus dying for all my sins. My heart softened when I remembered that "whosoever believeth in him should not perish, but have everlasting life." At that moment I sank to my knees by my bedside and confessed my sins, aware that Jesus died for all them, including the ones I could not even remember. My heart was melted as I prayed the sinner's prayer, because I knew that I now had the assurance of having everlasting life. I claimed that "whosoever" meant me too. When I thanked the Lord Jesus for dying for me, peace flooded my heart, and I knew He had forgiven all my sins and made me His very own.

As I stood to my feet, such peace flowed into my heart. I searched around for my Bible, which I had not read for months, and eagerly opened it up and began reading again in the Gospel of John. It was such a blessing to understand God's love, so much so that I could hardly blow out the lamp that night and on future nights as God was beginning to reveal His love and greatness to me through His Word.

All of a sudden, family prayers, church services and Bible studies on the radio began to mean everything to me. Later I joined the church choir, but strangely I had decided not to tell anyone about my conversion, as I wanted them to see that I was different and then ask me about it.

The clerks in my father's store began to tease me because I was singing all the time and they thought it was because of my cowboy. I thought to myself, *Can't you hear what I am singing*? I sang "What a Friend We Have in Jesus" and songs like that.

I had gone forward in a revival meeting when I was nine years old. I remember how I felt that Satan was holding me to my seat, but I finally got up and ran forward. I cried and prayed for forgiveness and even apologized to my parents and grandparents for things I knew I should have confessed. But my "conversion" did not bring a real change in my heart; I had not fully trusted in Jesus.

All that week after I had made a real commitment, I voraciously read my Bible. My mother came into my room one evening to try to see what I was reading. As I heard her footsteps, I quickly hid the Bible under the quilt. I just wanted her to see that I was different and ask me why.

The next Sunday night when we had family prayers, I was so thrilled with the Bible story that Dad read and with their prayers that when it was my turn to pray, instead of reciting the Lord's prayer as usual, I forgot and prayed extemporaneously from my heart. I ran to my room right afterwards, knowing that I had given myself away. My mother followed me and asked me, "Lil, what's happened to you? Are you saved?"

"I hope so," I smiled gently.

"To hope so, isn't enough," my mother pressed on. "You have to know so."

"But mother, I *know* so!" I said as I burst into tears.

After waiting for me to compose myself, mother then asked why I had not told them of the news. "Lil, I have been watching you during the past week and thought that you seemed to be different."

"That's what I wanted you to see," I sobbed through my tears of joy.

Then Mother said, "Let's go to Dad in the bedroom and share the news with him and thank God together."

BURIED WITH HIM

As I read my Bible I realized that baptism was a very important step in the Christian life. So I asked the church leadership if I could take this great step of faith. Like all the other candidates, I had to go before the whole church so that the members would have the opportunity to ask us questions or bring up any incidents that they felt should be confronted. My prayers were answered and they did not confront me at all.

The day of the baptism drew near and the weather was beautiful and sunny. I will never forget standing in the water—my church believed in total immersion—as the pastor spoke. It seemed as if the sky was filled with God's glory. I happened to glance up at the overlooking hill, and standing there was Harry, a fellow from school who had teased me unmercifully about being "holier than thou," for I was the first in the group to become a Christian. Harry was perched on his horse after traveling the ten miles from his home. He had taken off his hat and had rested it on the horse's head as he reverently watched me be baptized.

Several months later, after hearing on the radio about Briercrest Bible Institute, an interdenominational college in Caronport, Saskatchewan, along the Trans-Canada Highway, midway between Calgary and Winnipeg, I wrote off to them and requested more information about enrolling there. The brochure for the college explained that the educational institution had been set up to equip students to "minister

Daily Vacation Bible School Under the Canadian Sunday School Mission In Northern Saskatchewan

to the church and society by preparing them to think, value, live and serve in accordance with biblical principles." I liked what I read and so I applied and was accepted.

When I arrived at Briercrest, who should I meet but Harry? To my surprise, two weeks later, he accepted Christ as his Savior and was able to attend the Bible school. When he graduated from Briercrest, he became a member of the staff and served there all through his life. Some of his children later became missionaries.

How I loved my time as a student at Briercrest. The teaching was of a high standard and I received great new revelations from God's Word. I also made many wonderful new friends there. I was invited to sing in the quartet for the college radio program. In the summertime I would teach children the good news at a daily vacation Bible school in areas of northern Saskatchewan where there was no church or Christian witness.

The two years I spent at Briercrest were both inspirational and also challenging for me to become more personally involved in missions. I had wanted to be ready to share God's love wherever He called me and this had been a great stepping stone.

My life was indeed moving in an exciting new direction. But where would it end up? That had yet to be decided in heaven!

Chapter Three

ALL CHANGE

We were in for a big surprise when one day my father called a family meeting in the sitting room of our home. When he saw that we were all seated comfortably, he began his announcement.

"As you know," he started in, "things have been very difficult with the business here in Main Centre over the past few years. The Depression has hit us hard, but also the weather is so extreme that my health has suffered. Doctors here have said that both Sam and I need a change of climate to return to good health."

He glanced around the room to make sure we were all listening, then continued. "I have been making some inquiries, and I want you to know that your mother and I have made a decision."

My father stopped again for a long, agonizing moment while we all held our collective breath. *What is he going to say next?* we wondered.

"We have reached our decision. We are going to move to British Columbia," he announced. "The weather there is much milder. We have chosen the town of Abbotsford to live in, and you will be glad to know that they have a nice Mennonite church there."

None of us spoke. We were stunned. I suppose we had thought that nothing would ever change with our pleasant little lives and now it was *all change*!

We were to pack up and leave our town, our friends, our school, our church, and start again in a completely different area. I realized that I would not be able to return to finish Bible college in Briercrest. As a compensation, I knew we would have mountains and ocean instead of the prairies, so this was big news!

Seeing our confusion, my father went on to say, "My parents had to come all the way from Ukraine. I am just taking you to another province."

We all packed up our lives in a few boxes and suitcases and set off in Dad's van to a small farm on the edge of Abbotsford, which turned out to be a mix of rural and small-town urban neighborhoods. Located in the Fraser valley, it was just thirty-five miles or so outside of the impressive city of Vancouver.

My father had sold his business and began his new life managing a grocery store in Abbotsford. He later went on to sell real estate there. The family began attending the South Abbotsford Mennonite Brethren Church. We children all worked in a salmon cannery or picking hops and berries.

Having made one big move, I decided soon to make another. I took a job at the huge Simpson's department store—which later became Eaton's—in downtown Vancouver. Near the city hall and not too far from the store was the Metropolitan Tabernacle, which, I understand, was named after the church of the same name in London, England, that had been pastored by Charles Haddon Spurgeon, the "Prince of Preachers." This Canadian version was pastored by a Scotsman, William Robertson, who had been a pastor in a Liverpool church that also carried the Metropolitan Tabernacle name. I really enjoyed Pastor Robertson's sermons and was soon a part of the church choir. I also volunteered to teach in the Sunday school, was president of a girl's club, and very active in the young people's group. It was through the church that I also began helping at the Soldiers, Sailors and Airmen's Christian Association in Vancouver, where I had met Lloyd.

The war in Europe was still raging during this time and my brother John was stationed in England with the Royal Canadian Air Force. This was one of the reasons that I had begun helping at the Christian military association.

As I continued to work in the department store in Vancouver, I kept feeling the Lord reminding me of my com-

Metropolitan Tabernacle Young Peoples' Outing, when Marcus Robertson and Lillian were President and Vice President

mitment to missions, and I realized I needed to finish my Bible training that had begun at Briercrest. So, after some years, I applied to the Bible Institute of Los Angeles and was accepted.

Then I faced a huge hurdle. Because it was just after the war, I was told that it would be difficult to get a work permit to go to the States. Some friends I knew had waited six months and still could not get it. I resorted to believing

Soldiers, Sailors, Airman's Christian Assoc. party

prayer and during my lunch hour headed for the Canadian and US consul's offices in Vancouver. Instead of the battle that I had anticipated, the visa officer I spoke with processed my request in record time, once he had heard my reason for wanting to go to the States. Just twenty minutes after I had entered the office, I had the visa in my hand.

As graduation time drew near at BIOLA, I continued to agonize over what I should do regarding Lloyd and our future together. Should I marry him or go to India without him? I still was not sure and I was being torn apart with this decision. Night after night I found I could not sleep. I kept pleading with God to reveal His clear call to me from his Word regarding India or marriage.

I had arranged to visit my parents for Christmas in Abbotsford. Lloyd had asked me to break my journey in Seattle to stay overnight with the Buchards, his godparents. When I arrived at their home, they gave me a wonderful welcome. After dinner I noticed that Mr. Buchard had set up a projector and screen in the living room.

"We'd like you to see some of the slides that Lloyd took during his visit to see us," he explained. My heart dropped, as I knew that I could not face seeing them.

I excused myself and told them that I needed to go to my room as I had an "important decision" to make. They understood, for they seemed to sense the struggle that was taking place in my heart.

On my knees in that bedroom, with my Bible open before me, I reached out to God as never before. I could not stand to wait any longer. I had to know what God wanted for my life. I looked up all the verses I knew on evangelism, such as Matthew 28:19, Mark 16:15 and Acts 1:18. They all said in essence the same thing—"Go ye into all the world and preach the gospel . . ." I reminded God of John 3:16 and the time when He had narrowed the "world" down to me. "Now could You perhaps speak from that same verse to send me out to the world with that message?" I prayed. But it all just said the same.

I then began to flutter the pages aiming for the Psalms where I knew there were answers to nearly all the questions of life. In desperation I cried out, "Lord, You must speak to me clearly tonight. I cannot stand it any longer! Please show me in Your own words that You want me to go to India. Speak tonight or I will forget all about India and I'll marry Lloyd."

I looked down, and there in my open Bible, in what appeared to me to be raised, bold black letters, were the words of Isaiah 42:6, "I the Lord have called thee in righteousness. . . . " I held my breath. He had spoken. It was clear. Now if I did not go, I would be disobeying Him and I knew He had a right to my life.

I was glad, but now I had to write Lloyd about this. How could I do it? I read on: "I will hold thine hand . . ." I cried out, "Lord how can You hold my hand? I can't see You!" I then said to God, "Lord if You can give me the courage to go to India alone—and please give Lloyd someone who is even more worthy of his love than I am—then I am all Yours."

God had been waiting for surrender from me. Such peace and assurance began to flood my soul. I knew He was able!

"And will keep thee . . ." *In the heat of India.* This was important as I had found it very difficult to stand the heat of southern California. *The diseases and difficulties of a different culture. The money needed for support and travel. Language school and all the other needs.* He would keep me!

"And give thee for a covenant of the people . . ." I did not quite understand that until people heard about my call and promised to pray for me and to send support as God enabled. I have never had to ask for help, but God has always supplied my every need.

How wonderfully he proved this over and over again. I remember on one furlough I was in Everett, Washington, speaking at an evening meeting. I was staying with my friend Verona Hanson, who had been my roommate in Briercrest Bible Institute.

The next morning a lady who had been at the meeting came to see me. She told me that God had spoken to her at the meeting and shown her that she was to help support me with twenty dollars a month. I told her that my support was all in, but I was concerned about support for our Indian sisters on the staff, and I asked her if she would consider having it go towards that. "No," she said, "the Lord clearly told me it was to be for your support." So I asked her to send it to the mission headquarters in Philadelphia.

When I arrived in Vancouver that day, I heard that one of my supporters who had been giving twenty dollars a month towards my support had passed away. How wonderful—His promise "to keep" never fails!

"For a light of the Gentiles . . ." I knew that meant India and how I prayed that He would help me be *a light to India for Him*!

After this experience I wrote to Lloyd, explaining my position. I had a blessed Christmas with my family and then returned to BIOLA. Graduation time was drawing near. I had been taking a Christian education course there, as I had always been interested in being a teacher, and now I knew it had to be in India.

I had become overwhelmed with concern and sympathy for the many orphans in India. I loved children and had hoped to have my own—and maybe I would.

I was wearing a black cap and gown on that January day in 1948 at the BIOLA graduation ceremony that was held at the Church of the Open Door. With my parents and brother John, who had recently returned from his overseas service in Europe, looking on, I was presented with my certificate by Dr. Louis Talbot, the president.

I then had to travel to Philadelphia for an interview with the North American board of the Pandita Ramabai Mukti Mission. But even before the interview could take place, I was asked to work as a probationary missionary prospect at the Philadelphia headquarters, so the staff there could observe me at close quarters. My main task was to do the cooking in the home for the general secretary and the staff.

This was a real test for me, as I had never done much cooking before. My mother had taken care of that for years, and I had been out working or studying for so long that I had not had much opportunity to learn the skills of cooking.

One thing I could do, however, was to make good pies for dessert. I was always glad when company came as they seemed to appreciate the food and would especially compliment me on my good pies.

The staff at the house rarely handed out compliments for my cooking, or anything else, for that matter. This tactic seemed to be part of a test to see how I worked.

When it came time for the interview with the board, I had done a lot of praying before I went before them. It turned out to be a time that was not as strained as I had thought it would be. In fact, they were most friendly. Still, I was glad when it was over. At the end of the formal interview, I was told to wait outside while they made a decision about my application.

After a few painful minutes, the general secretary came out and, with a smile, told me, "Lillian, I am glad to tell you that you are accepted as a missionary for the mission. But you probably won't be going to the field for another year. We need somebody to replace the missionary principal of the school going on furlough. We want you to delay for twelve months before you go to India and get your teacher's training certificate to be able to fill in the position of principal of the Mukti school." I was happy, for I had always wanted to be a teacher, too.

The year went quickly. I took classes during the day, preparing for the teacher's certificate. Saturdays and holidays I worked at Eaton's department store. In the evenings I did babysitting to take care of my accommodations. Two evenings a week were spent in the Shaunessy area of Vancouver at the home of Ralph and Bernie Kemprud, friends from my church. Ralph was a builder and their three children—Ed, six; Audrey, five; and Meryl, two—were delightful company. They took in the stories from the Bible that I read to them and the mission's *Buds and Blossoms* stories, which always thrilled them. I remember one evening when both Ed and Audrey prayed to ask Jesus to come into their hearts.

Eventually, these children became faithful supporters of the ministry, not only for me, but also for the girls in the mission, with money from the very first newspapers they sold, the jobs they had through their school and college training.

LLOYD'S FUTURE

Three months after Lloyd and I had broken up, and after I had been praying that he would find a "worthy" life partner, I received a letter from him in which he told me that he wanted to share with me what God had done for him. I felt my eyes begin to mist up as I read his words:

Lil, I could not pray the prayer you asked me to pray at first. But I finally made the request to the Lord to lead me to the one he had for me. One morning a lady came to my church in Toronto and I welcomed her and found her a seat. Later on, when the service had started, the only seat left for me was the chair behind her. I have to confess that I can't remember a word that the pastor said during his sermon that morning. I just kept thinking, *Is this the one for me?* But then I thought, *Oh, you fool. Maybe she is a married woman. You never looked to see if she had a ring on her finger.*

After the service, I stood at the door shaking hands with people and inviting them back for the evening service, when she came by again. It was then that I noticed that she had an engagement ring on, but it was on her right hand. This meant that either she had a broken engagement or it was the ring of her mother or grandmother.

I invited her back for the evening service and sure enough that evening, she was there. After the service, when we went for fellowship at one of the homes, I went along. I was surprised to find that my friend's wife had seen this new lady in the church and had invited her also to come and had even brought her along.

So that evening, we became acquainted and Lil, you won't believe this, but I even stopped by at my home and introduced her to my mom. She thinks she is wonderful and I am sure she is the one for me. Her name is Grace.

I felt so happy for both of them. However, I was surprised, because Lloyd had an English background and was on the conservative side. For this to happen so quickly to him was nothing short of a miracle. He and Grace were married shortly afterwards.

It was astonishing how my support came in. I had told the Lord that I would never beg for money, but I wanted to trust Him to keep me as He had promised. Slowly, but surely, it all came in.

Now came the time for me to hand in my resignation to the floor manager of the big department store where I had been working. The manager came to me and asked sharply, "Miss Doerksen, why are you leaving us?"

"To go to India to work with orphans," I replied.

He scratched his head and looked puzzled. "What's the deal? I hope it's worthwhile. How much are they paying you?"

"They are paying me nothing," I explained. "It is what we call a faith mission."

Before I could go on, he swore and asked, "What in the #%*#! is a faith mission?"

When I explained it to him, he said, "Oh, Miss Doerksen, don't be a fool and throw away your life with something like that."

I threw back my shoulders and said, "Mr. Davenport, if the God who has called me to India isn't even a greater employer than Sir Timothy Eaton for whom I am working now, then He's not worth serving. But I know that the God who has called me is great and will supply all my needs."

The man seemed to be a little nervous. "Well, well, well," he stuttered. "More power to you, but keep in touch."

I promised that I would and it brought some surprising results. I was so surprised when he sent several donations through one of the clerks who had worked with me. I did not have time for personal letters on the field, but I sent him my newsletters regularly.

When I came home on furlough I went to visit Ellen, the clerk who had sent donations for him, who had started a shop of her own . When I got there, who should I see but Mr. Davenport, who had also dropped in to see her? I hardly recognized him for he seemed so changed. He was happy to see me and told me, "Miss Doerksen, you will be glad to know that I'm going to church now." What a happy visit we had!

Chapter Four

PLEASE SANCTIFY MY SMELLER

The big moment had finally arrived. It was time for me to leave for India, the world's second most populous nation, after China. In late September of 1950, I faced farewells and parting from my family and friends with mixed feelings. The Lord's promise through His Word that He was "holding my hand" and "keeping me" brought comfort and also assurance from God to my beloved parents.

When I arrived at the Vancouver Canadian National Railways (CNR) Station to catch the train to the American East Coast, a crowd had already assembled to bid me farewell. I was finding it hard to keep control of my emotions as they followed me to the platform where the train was waiting and began singing, "God be with you 'til we meet again."

Leaving for the Railway Station in Vancouver to Go to New York and Sail to India—November 1950

It was nearly time for the whistle to blow and I was bravely saying good-bye to all of my friends and trying to console my mother, when suddenly I noticed that my favorite little sister, five-year-old Sylvia, was not there. "Where is she?" I asked, but no one seemed to know. I did not care if I missed the train. I had to see her. While others were searching the platform, I ran into the waiting room and I found her in a corner weeping her heart out. She could not bear to see me go. Lovingly, I brought her back to the train. Only a few more minutes remained for a final farewell to my friends and family and my lovely Sylvia. The whistle blew and we were off. I stood on the step of the huge train waving good-bye.

Farewell at Vancouver CNR Station. Dad, Mom, Sisters, and Brothers

Most of my family and friends were crying, but I had managed to control myself. As I had gotten onto the train, I had put myself into the hands of the Savior who had called me and felt Him hold my hand. The long journey, that took me through the Canadian Rockies and then down through the States, eventually ended for me in Philadelphia, my destination.

After a couple of days at the mission headquarters there, I was taken to a big freighter in New York on October 4, 1950. When I got into my cabin I had another touching experience. I knew that I was leaving my country for a land that would be very different from mine. I suddenly realized that I was going alone on a six-week ocean trip. Loneliness swept over me and I almost felt like jumping off the ship and returning to Canada. Then I looked in my cabin and saw bouquets of flowers and messages that had been sent from home and I knew that they were praying for me. Suddenly, the cabin was filled with the presence of the Savior who was holding my hand. It was a dramatic moment for me. I saw the love of God in all the flowers and messages that had come and was comforted.

The moon was shining at half-mast as we pulled out of Brooklyn at 2:15 in the morning. I stood on deck and watched as we passed by the Statue of Liberty, heading out towards the Atlantic. Soon the lights of the "Big Apple" began to fade and sink into the horizon and I went to my cabin.

The next morning I got up feeling wonderful, but that did not last long. With the rocking of the ship I promptly lost the breakfast I had just eaten. To make matters worse, the weather changed and the ship began tossing and reeling as the wind and rain lashed the deck wildly. We had to stay in our cabins all day.

By October 10, we were 2,343 miles from New York and 2,885 miles from Beirut, our first port of call. The weather had begun to calm down a little and soon the blue sky had replaced the angry dark clouds. We could start sleeping again without fear of falling out of our bunks.

The sea lost its beauty again when the storms came up and we were tossed in our cabins and could hardly get to the rail to take care of the seasickness. When we passed Gibraltar and went through the Mediterranean, we were glad to know that we were nearing Beirut.

On our way to the Red Sea, there was a terrible, unexpected storm on the Mediterranean. Suddenly, while we were having our lunch, the ship lurched and we were thrown into one another's laps. All of the dishes and food went smashing to the floor. With difficulty, the staff helped all of the sixteen passengers on board to our cabins.

On the ship we had Sunday meetings and it was interesting to see the expressions of the crew and the passengers as we shared from the Word of God and about His leading in our lives. Two other missionaries and I would take turns in leading the meetings. Hours were spent on the deck, reading the Word of God and writing letters. The other passengers and crew were wonderful, as was the captain. They all seemed interested as I shared with them about my life. This made the days pass quickly.

The captain would tell me stories about how the merchants on the streets of Bombay sat on the counters of their stalls playing with their toes and then serving one and all with food. These things did not comfort me, but prepared me in a way for what lay ahead.

At Beirut, Lebanon, we were able to disembark. I suddenly realized that this was to be an introduction for a whole new way of life that was really a million miles from what I was used to in Canada.

The narrow, dirty streets were filled with boys carrying large trays of food on their heads and noise was everywhere. It was both exciting and disconcerting at the same time.

A group of us managed to persuade a taxi driver to take us to Damascus in nearby Syria. The trip was beautiful, with the taxi winding in and out of the lovely mountains and valleys terraced with grape vineyards, olive and fig groves. We passed Mount Hermon, where Jesus fasted for forty days. It was hard for me to take in that His sacred feet had actually climbed these rugged paths.

When we arrived in Damascus, I was amazed to see the people were wearing the same style of dress that I am sure was worn in Bible times. Walking along the narrow streets of the bazaars that our Savior trod, with people crashing into you all the time, was incredible. There were also donkeys and camels. All mingled to make up an atmosphere that I will never forget. We came to the biblical "street called Straight" and later saw the window through which Paul was let down in the city wall gates. We also saw the road along which he had hurried away that night. There was the house where Saul went when he was blinded by the light and Ananias came and touched his eyes and Saul gave himself to Christ. Soon it was time to return to Beirut and resume the journey.

Eventually, after a marathon trip that stopped in Saudi Arabia and Pakistan, we finally arrived in Bombay, India's main port that lies midway along the west coast of the country on the Arabian Sea. It was hard saying good-bye to everyone on the ship. We had become such good friends.

I was met on board there by Bhimabai, the headmistress of the Mukti school and also Jean McGregor, the principal. We went to the custom's shed to get my baggage cleared and then once that was done, we were to have a meal. At last I was in India, the world's largest democracy, walking the jammed streets of historic Bombay—"good bay" in Portuguese. Many believe Bombay will be the world's most populous city by the year 2,020 with some fifteen million people packed in there like sardines.

I marveled at the strength of the sinewy men with sweat on their faces who were pulling the handheld pull carts that carried everything from glass to books and even hot meals from one end of the city to the other. There were beggars, hawkers, all kinds of humanity and wandering cows in huge numbers that I had never seen before.

They then took me to Victoria Terminus, Bombay's main railway station, and to the dining room in this edifice that is considered to be one of the finest railway stations in the world. I was told that it served English food; they had taken me there so I would not have to worry about the hot spices of the usual Indian fare. We had soup and were halfway through the meal when suddenly tears began to run down my cheeks and my nose ran, as I was overwhelmed by a wave of nausea. My companions were worried, thinking I was homesick.

"No, it's this food," I explained as my face twisted up. "It's so spicy."

"But, it's very mild," insisted Miss McGregor. "That's why we came here."

So I tried to finish it. I had once had a bad experience with Indian food in Canada

Greeted by Beth Stone and Coolie—Arrival at Kedgaon Station

that had caused me to have severe uneasiness for days. Then I realized that what had caused the problem was the smell of the clarified butter that had soaked the orange papers in which the sweets they served us were wrapped. This awful smell had saturated my "smell buds."

I felt a sense of excitement when we went for a short walk along the bazaars and stalls on the crowded and noisy streets and alleys of Bombay. I had never before seen so many people pressed together in one place. As we passed the food vendor's stalls where they were frying up all kinds

of food, clouds of steam and smoke snaked up towards the sky past me. I recognized again the food was also being fried in clarified butter for the crowds around each cart. This putrid, spicy smell so enveloped me that I knew I could never stand it. I stood still, and right there in desperate earnestness, pleaded

In Mukti "Taxi", Arriving at Mukti Gate

with God to "sanctify my smeller" or I would have to go back on the same ship to Canada. I felt I could do this as my baggage was still on the wharf and the ship would be returning in two days.

No More Smells

Right there, God took my sense of smell away. To this day I can smell nothing bad or pleasant. But I can taste! What a miracle!

After picking up my luggage back at the wharf, we went back to the Victoria terminus to catch the train to Kedgaon, an overnight journey. I was overwhelmed as I faced the challenge of the children of India for the first time on the station platform. I was surrounded by hungry, half-clothed, dirty, lice-infested children pleading so pitifully for food. It made my heart ache with compassion.

When our train arrived, we clambered into a second-class compartment for five. It was 11:00 P.M. as the train moved away from the station with the wheels clanking heavily against the tracks and the carriage shaking fiercely. I was shocked when one of the two men who were sharing the compartment with us suddenly stripped off in front of us and got into his nightclothes. I did not sleep a wink in the upper bunk that night and I was ready to fight them off if they came near me. But it was a quiet night.

Greeted by Kamal and Girls in Mukti with Flowers and Garlands

My arrival and welcome will always be a precious memory for me. The missionaries from Mukti met me at the station with garlands and we traveled in the blazing sun to the mission in the Mukti taxi—a covered bullock-cart pulled by two big, white bullocks who lumbered down the track to the front gates of the property. There, some 800 girls and women were waiting for me with radiant, clean faces and a happy welcoming song. I discovered later that all of these had been destitute, unwanted, half-starved sick or beggar children who had been rescued, and at Mukti they were loved and cared for. This challenge was to remain with me when others like them came. The garlands, flowers, songs and hugs given by the little ones (called *buds* and *blossoms*), teenagers, women and staff will always remain in my heart.

HOME AT LAST

The next day I was taken on a tour of the mission and saw the nursery with its hanging cradles and the compounds where children, teenagers, women and blind of all ages, lived. I had finally come home. The visit to the nursery was a special blessing. The cradles from which the babies were hanging from the ceiling were made by orphan boys that Ramabai cared for before a home for boys was started in another place. The ropes by which the cradles hung were made by blind women in the blind workroom. The young girls who were looking after the babies had once lain in those cradles themselves.

As we turned to leave the nursery, Dellibal, the senior matron in the nursery, whom the founder had trained, put her arm on my shoulders and said sweetly, "*Moushi*, we have chosen a name for you."

Ramabai called the missionaries who came to work with her, Moushi, which means "mother's sister."

She went on to explain some of the other names. There were the *Suwartha Moushi* (Evangelistic Auntie) and *Stuti Moushi* (Praise Auntie) and others.

"We have chosen for you the name *Prakash Moushi*."

When I asked her what it meant, she replied, "It means the 'auntie of light.'"

Tears came to my eyes. It was a confirmation from the Lord that He would help me to be a little light in this wonderful place.

When we visited the Blind school, home and the workplace for the blind, they surrounded me with loving hugs. The little girls put their hands all over my face and body to get to know me and asked me questions in the Marathi language which was interpreted, so they could learn what I was like. When I saw some of the girls on the side chattering excitedly, I asked my interpreter what it was all about. She asked them and they told her that they had chosen a name for me.

I told them I had already been given a name and asked what name they had chosen. They told me happily that I was going to be their *Tejasweni Moushi* (bright-light auntie).

I was touched. It was a double confirmation from the Lord that He would help me to shine for Him, for that had been my deepest prayer.

Chapter Five

THE PLACE
OF THE PALMS

T he sun was already shredding away the morning mists as the village postman, bearing a bag full of mail for us, came into view at the front gate of the mission property. He seemed the perfect person for me to practice my Marathi on.

"Postman, I'm Miss Doerksen," I called out in English. He stopped in his tracks and then came over towards me as I sat on the broad verandah by the front gate with my notes in front of me. I was feeling confident that I was beginning to master the intricacies of this new language. I took a deep breath and launched into my question to him.

"*Kay ahe? Mala putra pahije,*" I said proudly, thinking I was asking if he had a letter for me. A look of disgust swept his face and he did not seem to know how to respond. My *pandit* (Indian-language teacher) who was sitting with me gasped in surprise. Then he explained with a chuckle, "Moushi, you have just asked him if he has a 'son' for you?" He explained that *putra* is son and *patra* is letter. I never forgot that linguistic lesson.

The poor mail carrier shook his head in disbelief and then went about his business. "It's back to the drawing board for me," I said to myself, blinking my eyes against the sunlight.

Because of this faux pas, I vowed that each day I would work even harder at my language studies. My pandit and I would sit at a table under the trees or in a room by the front gates as he patiently tried to impart his linguistic knowledge of this complicated language to me. Each night I would sit up late beside the flickering kerosene lantern that cast eerie shadows across my simple room, preparing my lessons for him for the next day.

Besides my studies, I was also assigned duties in the superintendent's office where I dealt with the admissions and departures of Mukti residents to and from the Mukti Mission. It was a place for needy Christian girls and women.

A year and a half later, when I passed all of my language exams, I was appointed principal of Sharada Sadan, the primary school and kindergarten for 300 orphan and village children. I was also given oversight of the home of Elim Sadan, which means "The Place of the Palms." It was the boarding hostel for court-committed girls and also girls from poor Christian families. When it grew into a large family of over sixty girls, I found my days were more than full with all my responsibilities, which included dealing with very difficult girls.

I did have one big breakthrough, however. I learned to tell all the girls apart. Initially, I had found it to be an almost impossible task, as all of them had long black braids and dark eyes. Now I began to know who was who and could even remember their names.

ANUSAYA JOINS US

We never knew who would be the next to join our community. One Saturday, I was called by a guard to the gate and there it was I first met Anusaya, a bright-eyed, five-year-old, with her wizened, old granny at her side. The old woman, whose brown skin was a thick as leather, explained with tears in her eyes that betrayed the inner pain that she was feeling, that Anusaya's father had died and her mother was dying of tuberculosis.

"There is no one left for care of her," she said sadly. "I am just too old to look after her. Would you please take her?" I tried to imagine the inner struggle that this dear life-worn Indian woman must be dealing with and so I smiled gently and said, "Of course, we will take her."

The grandmother nodded in gratitude and then turned over to me all the little girl possessed, namely, two tiny, shriveled up mangoes and a small ball of food tied in a dirty, gray rag. With that she left, and I looked at this sweet little girl before me. I could see that her eyes were black and alive to everything. I also noticed at a glance that her head was alive, too!

When I brought her into our Place of the Palms, most of the other girls received her gladly. After her bath they gleefully joined in the search for those little "traffic officers" in her hair.

One girl, however, was reluctant to receive Anusaya into our tight-knit family. Goony, our other five-year-old, wondered for a day or so whether she wanted to share her privileges and affections as the youngest of our family with another. Fortunately, she soon realized that her new little sister would be wonderful company and that she could teach her lots of things.

As I observed Anusaya at close quarters, I realized that although she was only five years old, she must have been a fine cook, and had apparently been able to help her mother when she had lived at home. For she would pick leaves and sit down beside a flat stone, fold back her little dress and roll and rock another smooth stone on the leaves exactly like all Indian village women prepare their vegetables. When the leaf was exactly the right texture, she would place it in a little plate of water. Anusaya would then look up at me, smile, and then answer whatever question I would ask her. She would go right on working as though there was nothing as important as getting the meal prepared on time.

PLANTING TIME

It was planting time at the Place of the Palms. Everywhere you could see new seedlings and saplings. Each one of the girls knew by heart that our scriptural theme for the Place of the Palms was found in Isaiah 61:3: "That they might be called trees of righteousness, the planting of the Lord, that he might be glorified."

The girls' dark eyes were wide, alert and eager as we began. My head would spin with the conversations that took place during this time.

"Let's plant this one here."

"Moni, water these."

"Watsala, don't pull up that one. It's not a weed, it's a tree."

From early in the morning, the children's voices would ring as they planted, watered, trimmed, transplanted and weeded. Shortly after I began my new duties, we had a number of new trees planted in the compound.

How important these planting days had become. The children would faithfully tend their new trees and plants—not just when they felt like it, but every day. For we all knew that not for a single day could we afford to neglect these living trees that God had planted here for them to tend. I would tell them that we cannot make up tomorrow what we miss today in prayer and loving care.

These times in the garden would mean countless interruptions for me—"Moushie, may I have a ribbon or string for my braids?"

"Moushie, come make a swing."

"Could you please tie the skipping rope to the trees?"

"Did I get a letter?"

"It's my turn to cook in the morning. Please may I have the alarm clock, and will you set it for 4:30 A.M.?"

Some, who came from very unfortunate backgrounds, and were committed to us by the court, had many things to learn.

I remember Manu, a twelve year old who was always getting into trouble. She found it so difficult to obey instructions. After several reprimands and being given "one more chance or you will be punished," the matron called me and told me that I would have to take action. It was serious. I led Manu to the storeroom outside my room, closed the door and told her to consider what she had done. She was rude and showed no repentance. I knew that I would have to get out my strap.

I felt awful using the belt and almost cried when I took it down from the peg. I remembered my father's words when he had to punish me, "This hurts me more than you." I had not believed him and wondered why he had spanked me then.

Now I knew what he meant! I found it hard to go into that storeroom. After administering the punishment, I took her to my room and she was surprised to see my tears. I loved her before I prayed with her and she too had tears and apologized for her actions. I never had any problems with her again!

The most welcome interruption would come at 6:30 in the evening when one voice after another at my door would ask, "Isn't it time for prayers yet?" Soon the verandah would be a mass of crossed legs as the girls sat on the floor. We would have a message from our "Heavenly Planter" and then it was time for prayer requests. These would fairly tumble one upon the other as praise and petitions and intercessions would rise to the Throne of Grace. Often, this would take place to a spectacular rose sunset that would soon turn to lilac and lavender in the dusk. Night falls quickly in India, for there is no lingering dusk to soften the transition from day to darkness.

These times were precious, as well as morning prayers at dawn. Just as the red ball again began to reappear, the girls would slip into the room one by one to have their "quiet time" with the Lord. Maybe the nourishment received here caused their roots to be firmly and deeply planted in the Christ who redeemed them on the tree of Calvary. I hoped that the sap of joy and peace and praise would flow through their boughs to give refuge to many others in India who still knew nothing of the shelter of the Savior's love.

EVANGELISTIC CAMPS AND SUNDAY SCHOOLS IN THE VILLAGES

We really looked forward to conducting regular five-day camps in unreached villages. A group of us from Mukti would travel by bullock carts to these dark places where we saw hearts open up to the love of a living Savior. I would

Village Sunday School Meetings

lead a team of what we called our "Bible women," who were our native evangelists, as well as some of our House of the Palms girls. We would stay in tents and visit in the villagers' homes. We'd often leave during the full flame of the dawnlight, arriving in a blaze of silver at midday and to the scent of dung fires over which the cooking was done. We would visit homes in these villages and we would see hearts reach out in hope and faith to a Savior of love during our outreaches.

On those Sunday after-noons, I would look for-ward to a short siesta, then would take time to hike to the hills or a creek with our dedicated team.

During these "cru-sades," we were especially received in joy by the chil-dren who gathered on the verandah floor "polished" with cow dung, as we sang

Lil in Village—Sunday School Outreach

and shared the story of the living God.

One Sunday in our Sunday school in Kopodi, a village near the mission, while we were singing, "*Kiti chan ahe, bapacha ghari*" (In my father's house . . .), I spotted a grizzled figure of a man crawling to where I was leading the sing-ing. I could hardly believe my eyes when I realized that, because of leprosy, he had lost most of his fingers and his toes. I had heard how the bacterium invades the peripheral nerves, skin, and mucous membranes, damaging the nerves and causing anesthesia. This was why so many injuries go untreated and accounts for many of the deformities.

He turned his wasted face toward me. With hollow cheeks, his eyes stared from sunken sockets. Then he spoke. "Sing that song again. Where is that home?" he said in a voice that was barely audible.

I realized that because that he was ravaged with this dreaded disease, he wanted to know about this place that was so beautiful. With a heart that was overcome with com-passion, I explained the way of salvation to him. After we

"No Hope but Jesus." The Leper and His Wife Who Found Hope

had sung that song again, he said simply with a voice that was choking with emotion, "I want to go there!"

After the service the man asked me to follow him to his tiny shack. He literally crawled in front of me, past bleating goats, barking dogs and shouting boys, and led me to his wife, whom I was to discover was in an even worse condition than he was.

The following Sundays we would try to bring them some cheese and *chuppattis* (unleavened bread) and share and pray with them. But week after week as we visited that village, we noticed our dear old leper couple were becoming weaker and weaker. The ravenous disease had now even nearly robbed the man of both of his precious eyes. But our hearts were always warmed because of his warmth and his growing simple faith in his Savior.

One particular Sunday when we arrived, there was only deep concern in his face. The disease had suddenly launched a mad, open attack on his wife's body. In the week since we had last seen her, she had been reduced to skin and bone. He explained that their only means of even a meager existence was to beg in the village. She had been able to go and beg even when he found it impossible to leave their shack, but now she was not even able to do this.

The man's bare, spindly legs seemed even thinner than usual; each rib protruded on his shirtless chest. His concern, however, was not for himself. His wife, whose body had not shown the same outward marks of the disease, was suddenly breaking down and was also now in great distress.

He could not bear to see her suffer and he pleaded with us to "do something for her." We felt helpless. All we could do was to pray for her.

When we came the next time to the village, I noticed that the man had shuffled over to the place where we were singing and telling the people of the love of Jesus. I then noticed another villager sit down beside him and was shocked to hear what he said. Instead of encouragement and a bit of help, he deplored the poor leper's condition and asked him why he did not cook up a poisonous weed growing nearby and drink the juice to end his and his wife's misery.

We later rebuked the man for his heartlessness and followed the leper again to his home. We promised to bring some medical aid for them, and his faith was strengthened as we sang and prayed together with him and his wife.

Several days later the doctor and Bhimabai accompanied us, and this visit brought joy like a beam of sunshine to that humble bare shack. The doctor immediately realized that they were by now beyond any medical aid, but they were grateful for the salve and pills that would relieve something of their suffering

They had prayed that God would send them something to eat. It was obvious that malnutrition was aggravating the disease more and more. We had brought one of the tiny tins of cheese sent to us from America for those in need.

We opened it before them and they gratefully accepted the nourishment they so badly needed.

On the next visit, we found their condition had gotten even worse. Rain was streaming through the porous roof, which was made of sticks and mud. The poor man had broken out in other smelly sores and was hunched up in the only dry spot there. I gave him a sheepskin jacket to serve as a blanket to keep him warm. His wife lay near to him groaning, with only an old sari wrapped around her. Her hands and arms were raw and covered with flies. There was no bed in the hovel. How glad we were that the Lord had reminded us to bring a little bedding. He was cheered and comforted and he prayed so earnestly with us that his wife might share his faith in Jesus, their only hope.

All during that week, our group at the Place of the Palms continued to pray for this dear old woman, that she might come to share her husband's faith in the Savior, and his hope for an eternity in His glorious presence.

As usual on Sunday we had our little service in the village, and our two friends managed to stagger over to join us. When the meeting was over we had a little time to talk and pray with them. We greeted them cheerfully and turned to leave after placing a little food before them. I had just turned the corner when I heard the old man call out. At the same time I was struck with a conviction to return to speak with his wife about her soul.

I did this and asked her when she was going to trust in Jesus as her husband did. If her answer surprised me, the conviction with which she said it, impressed me even more.

"But Jesus is my Savior," she interrupted. "Have we anyone else but Him?" She then revealed that all day long she sang the chorus she had learned at our meetings. It was:

Jesus saves me,

Jesus saves me now,
Hallelujah, Hallelujah,
Jesus saves me.

When we went again the following Sunday, we had to tell them that there was no hope; there was nothing more that medicine could do for them.

"No hope?" he repeated, and his head fell on his breast. Then raising his disfigured face heavenward, he whispered, "No hope but Jesus. We have no one but Him." His face lit up with hope and joy. He said simply, "Come and go with me to my Father's house."

Tears came to our eyes as the old lady joined in with deep sincerity in the closing prayer.

Not long afterwards, both the leper and his wife went to be with their heavenly Father. The leper's last words were, "Lord Jesus, take me soon."

The Demon Possessed Woman

We had another dramatic experience in that same village. I never dreamed that I would encounter such a situation, although I knew that there were many cases of demon possession in this country.

A woman was in our path, screaming and beating her head against the ground. I was joined by others from Mukti to pray for her deliverance. It was wonderful to see the power of our Savior demonstrated, and a great witness to all to see the woman released as we called on the name of the Lord Jesus, and claimed deliverance for her.

Suddenly, she was in her right mind and told us that she had heard the gospel ten years previously and she knew that Jesus was the Savior. We discovered that she had become demon possessed shortly after hearing the gospel when she had refused to obey the light and had not destroyed her idols. She had eaten live coals in a trance and it had caused her mouth to become full of blisters. The moment we called on the Lord to deliver her, she had stopped her screaming, and she got up repeating the name of Jesus, saying that He was Lord.

We left her walking quietly to her house and prayed for her that she might be obedient to God, forsake and destroy all and follow the Savior alone in spirit and in truth. All the people were utterly amazed.

Yes, my early days in India were packed with incidents, so dramatic and worthwhile. It was truly frontline ministry.

SUNRISE WITH BILLY GRAHAM

Weeks of individual and united prayer followed the news that Billy Graham was to visit India in January of 1956. Prayer was most intensified as political riots threatened to hinder the blessing we longed to see in this land.

When the day of the first meeting in Bombay dawned, the riots were at their peak. Many groups of Christians en route to the meeting were forced to return home when train services were discontinued.

Several of us from the Mukti Mission had begun our journey the night before. We had been taken off the train in Poona when all trains were canceled. We stayed at the railway station overnight and as we prayed together we marveled because we felt no disappointment. There was a quiet assurance in our hearts that God was leading us. Suddenly, there was some excitement, and we were informed that one train was "going through." We were allowed to go at our own risk with no guarantee of arrival in Bombay. After twelve hours delay en route, we finally reached Bombay that night.

When we finally arrived at the only hotel where we could get accommodation, because a curfew had been imposed, it was midnight. We were told by the desk clerk that three of us would have to share one bed. On the elevator going up to our floor, we discovered that the men traveling up with us were members of the Billy Graham team who were staying at this hotel. They told us that we had missed the only meeting that would be held in Bombay.

"The big crusade meeting had to be canceled and Dr. Graham and the rest of us team members are leaving by plane at dawn," one of them added.

We wondered if our hopes had been in vain, but they told us they would inform Dr. Graham and would try to arrange an interview for us before he left in the morning.

After we had retired to our room, a surprise ring on the phone announced the unexpected arrival of Beth Stone, the missionary who had been in charge of the Place of the Palms before me. She shared our room, too, sleeping on a settee, and the blessing we were to experience later that morning.

At 6:00 A.M., I was awakened by the shrill ring of the phone again invading the quiet of the room. It was one of Dr. Graham's associates informing us that Dr. Graham wanted to see us in fifteen minutes in the hotel lobby.

Overlooking the morning sea, we had our sunrise interview. With his piercing blue eyes, a face serene and radiantly shining with the love of Christ, Billy Graham, along with Cliff Barrows and Bob Pierce, the founder of World Vision, met with us. For a while that lobby was transformed into God's sanctuary. Dr. Graham had a message for us and for our churches from God's Word that went to our hearts. He encouraged us to be "patient in suffering, to continue to love one another, and be steadfast in our faith." Leaving us with a glimpse of the wondrous glory of Christ's appearing, he commended us in prayer to the Man of Glory.

It was not only the power and zeal of his message that marked Billy Graham as a man of God, but also his humility. This little meeting with us had seemed just as important to him as the huge multitudes that of late had gathered in other places to hear him. When he heard that some of our Mukti women in my Sunday school class had gone without their grain in order to contribute a gift of ten rupees to the expenses of his campaign in India, he felt it important

E. Stone, Dr. Marybai (AP Mission), E. Rohrer, Lillian, Billy Graham, Mrs. Howard (AP Mission), Bob Pierce

Leaving for First Furlough with Vimal Dongre, Newly Appointed Principal

to have a member of his team record the story, even though the contribution in material value was small.

It was a short, but wonderful meeting with the man who was to go on to see so many come to Christ in his extraordinary ministry, and it was one that none of us would ever forget.

As his bus and the police motorcycle escorts left for the airport, we waved him off with a prayer and sang, "Good-bye, our God is watching o'er you." I could see that he was moved as he waved back, his eyes shining with tears of joy.

Chapter Six

HONEYSUCKLE WONDERS

My first term at Mukti was full of interesting experiences. I had been working in the publicity office and the printing press, as well as in the village Sunday school. However, I feel my most rewarding and exciting story is what happened after my first furlough. For then I got my *Honeysuckle Wonders*!

When I had first arrived, the children in Mukti were all divided up in families by age groups. The nursery children, ages 1–6 were called the "Buds Compound"; then they graduated into the "Blossoms Compound," for ages 6–8; from there they went into the "Little Fruit Garden," ages 8–10; and then the "Big Fruit Garden," ages 10–12. The forty teenage girls were called the "House of Joy."

Coming from a large happy family, I along with some other missionaries, saw the need of dividing these girls into families of big and little sisters, to meet the needs of all the children. This way the little ones could get more attention, and the older girls would learn to help be responsible for the little ones. This idea was not well received by some of the older missionaries who felt that because the founder Ramabai had begun this compound system of age groups, and because it had been successful all through the years, it should not be changed.

However, one of the missionaries had pointed out that Ramabai had several thousand girls at that time. She accepted the questioning of others about whether it was wise to change the system that Ramabai had instituted. Still, this woman was not going to give up easily. She had tried several times to bring in changes, but was still facing opposition. I liked her ideas and I left on my furlough with this burden on my heart.

It was while I was in North America that I got the news that the "big change" had finally been achieved. All of the children were being divided into "flower families" of big and little sisters. Each family was named after a flower, such as the Sunflower Family, the Orchid Family, the Rose Family, etc. It was the ultimate in "flower power!"

My Mother's Passing

I was so grateful for the newly formed families and remembered how much my family had meant to me. We were close and I remembered that it was not easy for my mother to see me go so far away. I thought of the day when I was packing my trunks to leave for India. My mother suddenly came to the basement where I was preparing my clothes and other goods. I noticed that her lower lip was quivering. She looked sadly at me and said, "Oh Lil, we are going to miss you. Do you have to go so far away?"

I was surprised as she was a great prayer warrior and had a real heart for missions. She had seemed happy when I had initially shared with her that I had felt that God wanted me to be a missionary overseas.

"Mom," I responded gently, "you wouldn't want me to stay here when God has called me to India. You wouldn't want me to be out of His will, would you?"

"No, no," she said, wiping her eyes, "but India is so far away. If at least you were going out under our Mennonite Brethren Mission, we'd know you were all right, for I know the missionaries there are well cared for with good homes and cars and everything."

I looked up at her and was surprised with what came out of my mouth. "Mom," I interjected, "the Mukti Mission is about 800 or 1,000 miles away in another state from where the Mennonite Brethren Mission is located. You wouldn't want me even 800 miles out of God's will would you?"

She raised her head and shook it. Then my dear mother broke down and her tears began to flow freely as she said, "Of course not, Lil. Come on, let's pray."

I joined her on my knees as she poured out her heart to the Lord and then handed me over to the Lord to do His will, praying with deep emotion for my safe care and protection. With that my mother stood up, took out a handkerchief and gently wiped her eyes, and then hugged me close and went out of the room quietly singing.

When I returned to Canada on my first furlough after nearly seven years in India, it was a wonderful reunion for me to be with my mother and father as well as my brothers and sisters.

It appeared to be just a normal gathering, several weeks after I had come back. We were sitting in the living room of my parents' Abbotsford home, enjoying a cup of tea, as we entertained some dear friends who had come to the area for a conference.

After some small talk my mother said, "Lil, tell them about Kamal, our Indian daughter." They had been corresponding with a helper of mine.

My father had just been released from intensive care after surgery and was sitting across from us. Mother was sitting in her favorite chair as I enthusiastically started into the story. The words stopped in my mouth as all of a sudden I was startled to hear my dad shout urgently, "Mom, what's wrong?" His faced stamped with pain, he struggled up from his chair and moved towards where she was sitting. I quickly joined him.

I saw her chin drop and eyelids flutter, then her eyes close. By the time we reached her chair, she was gone. I turned my head to hide silent tears. It was such a shock for she was only sixty-two, and had been to the doctor not long before, and had appeared to be quite well. I had never seen death before and could not believe she had left us. Even now it is difficult to describe the depths of the sudden sorrow we all felt. She had been such a wonderful, loving mother and was my greatest prayer warrior and promoter. She had shared my letters and news of our ministry with everyone who came to the house and in the church prayer meetings. Her heart had been there with me.

I was comforted, however, that I would see my dear mother again one day in heaven. Still, I knew I would miss her terribly. After the funeral and thinking of going back to India, I asked Dad how I could possibly return without the backing of her believing prayers for me.

"We won't forget you," he assured me. "Lil, our prayers will be with you all of the time."

On my arrival back at Mukti, I found that the other staff members had all been allocated a "flower family," but there was none left for me. I was bitterly disappointed.

I shared my disappointment with Gladys Fletcher, the superintendent, who was a dear friend of mine. She and her brother had been brought up in boarding school because their parents were missionaries in India, so they had never really experienced family life. Gladys knew that I came from a big happy family so she came up with a temporary solution. She called me into her room one day and told me she was going to Australia on furlough and requested that I look after her Sunflower Family, helping them to become adjusted to family life while she was away. I happily agreed.

My Own Family at Last

When Gladys returned from Australia, she was happy with the way that I had run her "family." So she told me that I could now start my own family. I found it hard to cope with the excitement I felt as I heard her words.

"Oh Gladys, this is the most wonderful thing that could have happened to me," I said.

We started like a real family. I got six "leftovers" from the nursery and the matron who had looked after the Buds Compound, and so we grew like a normal family. Every year when new babies came to the door, we would have one or more, sometimes twins. The big girls would take care of the little ones.

We named it the "Honeysuckle Family" and we were the sweetest, happiest family you could ever imagine. We had wonderful times going on family outings and holidays and did many happy things together. There was always excitement with a new one joining our family.

It is wonderful to recall the stories of how these children came to us. One of our Bible women, an evangelist who worked in the villages and towns outside of Poona, was involved in one of them coming into our Honeysuckle Family. One morning, she went outside the place where she was staying and was shocked to see a little baby girl lying on the doorstep. She was dressed quite nicely and looked healthy. No one knew where the infant came from. The Bible woman who made the discovery got in touch with us immediately. We surmised that the child must have been left by someone who knew that in our Mukti home children were loved and well cared for.

When I saw this little mite, I loved her immediately. She was brought into our hospital nursery and the doctor there estimated she must be about six months old. She was kept in the nursery for special care for another six months. When she finally joined us, everyone loved her and we were so happy to have her in our family. I gave her a name—Madhubala (Honey Baby) and a birthday. She was beautiful and responded to the love and affection of her sisters.

Even though Madhubala was almost two before she finally spoke, she became one of the most brilliant girls in the family. In kindergarten, she quickly picked up both the Marathi and English songs and letters.

In fact, she did so well when she moved into our Sharada Sadan School (House of Knowledge) that she was at the top of the class. When several girls were to be sent to an English language medium boarding school, she and her Honeysuckle sister, Smrooti (Memory), with another Sunflower Family girl, were sent to a very fine Christian boarding school.

There she excelled in her studies, sports and music and went on to Wilson College at Bombay University. Madhubala was in her final year when a young man came from Canada to take back with him our baby Vidyulata, whom his parents had chosen to adopt on an earlier visit to Mukti.

While spending a month with us so Vidyulata could get to know him, he fell in love with Madhubala. Later I took her to Canada for marriage. However, as they got to know one another more, she realized that the marriage could not go through because their personalities were too different. She had to break the engagement and was able to get a scholarship and visa to go to Los Angeles to attend BIOLA College, from where I had graduated. There she earned another master's degree. She went to the Philippines for six months as a short-term missionary and then spent another year in Talbot Seminary.

Then she felt she owed a debt to return to India for service. The mission helped her to go to New York to prepare for a ministry with a mission called TAFTEE, where she was to revise the six-month Bible correspondence course in English. This was a six-month training program for her.

While Madhubala was in New York, she was required to minister to shopkeepers and students from India. She prayed earnestly for God to direct her for her future as her good looks were attracting many fine young men. During this time, a very fine young Indian man, who was a Christian studying at Cornell University, came into her life. He was nearing the completion of his Ph.D. in computer science. He had been praying for God to bring into his life a young woman—beautiful, brilliant, and Christian, who was also from India—and could be his marriage partner.

One day, he picked up a Christian magazine and he saw in it a picture of a lovely Indian girl and read her story. He was impressed and wrote to their office to ask for her address. They wrote and said she had been on their television program while she had been attending BIOLA University. He found out that she was in New York and was given the address of the Baptist pastor who was her supervisor there. He shared his desire with his own Baptist pastor who, coincidentally, knew the pastor in New York. The pastor encouraged him to send her a ticket so she could visit him and become acquainted.

She flew there and stayed in the pastor's home in Ithica and they spent the Saturday together. Then she flew back for the church service on Sunday in New York where she led the singing. After several visits, there was no doubt in either of their minds that God was leading them to spend their lives together. They wrote and phoned me in India and shared their assurance of God's will and Alex's desire to give her an engagement ring before she left for India.

I helped arrange the marriages of my girls, and felt that I did not want them to become engaged officially until I had met him. Yet I could understand his concern for her coming to India without a ring, for she was a very attractive young lady. Two months later, when I came home on furlough, who should meet me at JFK in New York but Alex with a beautiful red rose! It did not take long for me to see what a fine, suitable husband he would be for my Madhubala.

They were married soon after she returned from India after six months of service there. They now live in Virginia and have four wonderful and brilliant children, Joshua, Josiah, and the twins John and Jewel. To think what God had planned for that precious little doorstep treasure!

OUR LOTUS BLOSSOM

Kamal, one of our Mukti girls preparing for service, was a real help with the children. She would care for them when I had to be away and loved them dearly. She had the promise of a valuable worker, and became very close to me for she longed for a mother's love. I felt for her, especially when I remembered her story.

At one time our Bible women had gone to a well-known temple where thousands gathered for their religious festivals. While witnessing about Jesus near the temple, they saw a woman dart in and leave her little baby as a sacrifice to the gods. The Bible women were shocked and ran after the mother and told her not to leave the child, but she said that she had to. They quickly told her about Mukti where little children were taken in and loved and cared for and asked her if they could take her.

"Take her," she cried as she ran away.

The baby was brought to the mission and cared for with love and given the name Kamal (Lotus). She blossomed into a bright little girl with a beautiful singing voice and a desire to serve. When she finished high school and then seminary training, she felt called to give her life in missionary services in her home—Mukti.

OTHER HONEYSUCKLE WONDERS

Most days at the mission were filled with questions. Some easy to answer and others not so easy. Living in India had caused me to be prepared for anything, yet still my heart would ask why someone would abandon a young child and then leave.

Nurse Vimal asks, "Whose Baby is this?"

The big questions I tried to answer one day when I was called to the hospital were: who was this child? Where did she come from? What was her name? We did not know how old she was and we wondered where she came from. She had been left on an empty cot on the verandah of our Mukti hospital. When the staff nurse came and saw her on the bed, she asked the other mothers who were on their cots, "Who left this bed like this with no bedding on it? And whose baby is this?"

The mothers all said that they did not know. But the nurse knew that someone had put that tiny baby on the empty bed. The staff nurse looked around in the dispensary duty room, studied the roll call for the baby's name and questioned all of the helpers.

"Did someone bring this tiny baby for treatment?" she asked holding it up for everyone to see.

People just shook their heads.

She then asked Tatee, "Do you know anything about this?"

"About what?" asked Gaubay, the other helper, who was heating water over a low Primus stove on the floor.

"This baby, look!" the nurse said, pointing to the tiny figure.

Gaubay said, "Why, hasn't her mother come back yet? She put the baby on the empty bed and went out the back door. She said she would be right back."

But now that mother could not be found anywhere. The baby's abandonment was reported immediately to the doctor in the hospital and to the superintendent and they called the police who mounted a search for her. They combed the nearby market and the railroad station, but she was nowhere to be found.

The watchman had said he remembered a woman with a red sari and a nose ring running out of the gate. The wide search was in vain. Many questions were asked but not one was able to trace the mother or relatives of the little baby.

She was put in the baby's nursery where "nurse mothers" each took care of four or five babies. The nurse mother who took care of her had several very pretty little girls and this one was just an ordinary-looking baby, so she was neglected. Every time I went to the nursery for some work, I stopped by her cradle and she would beam from ear to ear and she looked sad when I had to leave.

One day when my matron-mother and I were in the nursery taking pictures of children and gathering information in order to write their stories, Ruth Akka, my Indian matron-mother, saw that the abandoned baby was being neglected. As we walked home, Ruth said, "Moushi, it's sad that little girl gets so little attention. How quickly she smiled when we went near her and touched her. She should be in a family."

Veerbala and Daniel with Honeysuckle Sisters, Anjali and Jayabala (LEFT), and Little Sister Stutibala (Prilla) with Her Adopted Mother

"Ours?" I asked hesitatingly, because we had just taken two other little ones into our Honeysuckle Family recently and she had her hands full.

"Yes," she said. "She needs love. God will help us to care for her."

So we chose this little infant for our Honeysuckle Family and called her Veerbala (Courage Baby).

The children were delighted and tried all day to get her to speak. As she grew, she still could not say a single word. Eventually, it finally happened. We were all gathered in my room on a Saturday night for our prayer and family devotional time and the other girls again tried to make her clap her hands as we sang.

She laughed and tried to clap her hands like the others and they were laughing and smiling with her. After we had begun the Bible study, we had such a surprise when suddenly we saw her turn her face to Ruth's face, on whose lap she was sitting, and clearly say, "Let's go home."

There were "aahs" from everyone and I could not believe my ears. "Did she really say that?" I asked Ruthie.

"Yes, she said it, I can hardly believe it," she answered. And from then on, you could not stop her talking. It seemed like a miracle and we were so thankful to God. Love had opened up all that she had stored up in her heart in silence. She grew up happily and was helping a missionary and his wife in Bangalore who had a Christian deaf school, while she attended a Bible college. Daniel, a young Indian man attending the seminary where this missionary also taught, came to their house one day and met her. He remembered her from the Bible college when he also attended. He fell in love and now they are fellow missionaries in charge of a large deaf church and school in the hills of South India. They also have two lovely young boys, Nathaniel and David.

HUNCHBACKED BIT OF MISERY TRANSFORMED

I will never forget the day when I saw her sit there on the hospital verandah, truly a hunchbacked bit of misery. Although she was over three years old, she only weighed fourteen pounds and could neither walk nor talk. My heart ached when I saw her. But I did not feel I could offer to take her into our family because I knew that Ruth, our little "mother" already had her hands full with sixteen little ones and one-and-a-half-year-old baby Madhubala (Honey Baby) who needed a lot of attention.

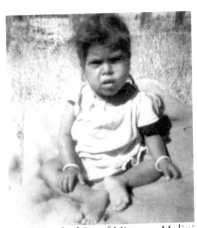

Hunchbacked Bit of Misery—Malini

I said nothing about my burden to Ruth and prayed that some other family would be willing to take her. But no one was. She was more than twice as old as our Honey Baby, but she weighed less than half as much.

Two days later she was still in the hospital waiting for somebody to take her. Ruth, who had heard about her, said, "Moushi, let's take her into our family. I know that I have my hands full, but God will give me strength."

I could hardly keep back my tears and assured her that God had a special blessing for those who were willing to deny themselves and for Jesus' sake were willing to love and care for such a miserable little mite.

When we brought the little girl into our home, sixteen wide-eyed youngsters between the ages of two and nine, sat on the floor of the room and began firing questions at me.

"Yes, Auntie, but her house? Was it like ours?" Suhasani (Laughter) gazed intently at her auntie's face as she asked.

"No, child, not like ours, I'm sure," I replied. "Her father died and the mother cannot find work. This three-year-old, who will soon be one of your sisters, did not have a proper place to live nor has she ever known what it means to have enough to eat. What is more, she can't even walk."

"Yes, but you said she is three years old. It will be a long time before our baby will be three and she can walk." Laughter looked more puzzled than ever.

"I'm so glad you reminded me, Suhasani. I wanted to explain about the walking.

"I think she does not walk yet because she has never had enough food. Her little legs are thin and shriveled-looking. When a baby is not properly fed, her legs just stay weak. Why, this little girl cannot even sit up properly and her back is all hunched."

Two-Year-Old Madhubala (Honey Baby) and Four-Year-Old Malini (Garland)

"Well, what shall we do with her then?" Cleanliness asked as she held out both hands palms up to express the despair she was feeling about the sister-to-be.

"That's exactly why I called you all together. I hoped that as a family we could think of what to do."

Fat, roly-poly Suwerna (Gold), the second youngest of the family jumped up, ready for action. "I'll give her a piece of my bread." Everyone giggled. Suwerna was never ready, at any time, to give more than a very little of anything that she herself could eat.

"I'll give her all my cereal," chimed in Tara (Star), amid more laughter.

"Yes, I know you Tara," I answered. "You and your morning cereal are forever enemies. But, food is very important if we are really to help this little girl."

"I guess that, if we gave her all the food in the whole world, she wouldn't get any better without God," declared Padma (Lotus). "I'm going to pray."

"Padma, you have thought of the very most important thing. We will need to pray God's special help in this situation for every single minute. And there is one more thing which bothers me about our new little sister. She doesn't smile or laugh as all of you do."

"I'll tickle her," declared Suwerna and her eyes danced as she practiced it on Honey Baby, who toppled over on the floor, abandoned to laugher.

Asha (Hope) watched in silence. Then all of a sudden she said, "Auntie, Suwerna shouldn't tickle the new little sister, should she? She is too sick to smile, I think."

"Perhaps you are right, Asha. You would not have laughed the day you came if we had tickled you. It took lots of prayer, a ride on the tricycle and a long walk with Suhasani to make you give us the tiniest smile, and you had been well cared for before you came. We will ask for special wisdom from God to find the right way to make this child laugh."

The discussion went on for some time. At last they tried to decide upon a name for the new sister. "Her name used to be Shalini, but we have a Shalini, don't we?" I asked, drawing a plump little six-year-old close to me. "What name has a similar sound so that she will not have too much trouble getting used to it?"

"Malini is similar, Auntie," suggested Ruth Akka, the matron-mother of the Honeysuckle Family.

"Yes, it is similar. It sounds good to me. Did you know that Malini means 'Garland?' Shall we name her Malini?"

"Yes," shouted a chorus of voices.

"I have been thinking that, though she seems a very sad little Malini at present, we could trust the Lord to change her into a real garland of joy for Him and for us."

The next morning a trip was made from the Mission hospital to carry little Malini to her new home. Every one of the Honeysuckles rallied around to try to help her fit into her new surroundings. Days and weeks went by. Every evening during family prayers they prayed for her, each child taking a turn: from the baby Madhubala, who repeated a little prayer after Ruth Akka, to Suwerna, then Tara, Yeshodhera (Holder of Success), Nilprabha (Purity), Ruth, Shalini (Purity), Asha , Padma, Suhasani and Nirmala (Cleanliness), all of whom prayed alone.

As a new bud in spring, Malini began to awaken. She showed the Honeysuckles that she understood everything they said to her by answering first with a word, then two, and finally with whole sentences. With a diet of good food, supplemented by cod-liver oil, iron and calcium, her little legs and back began to grow strong. She could sit up without that hunched forward look. She began to smile, then laugh. In every way she could, she responded to all the love and attention showered upon her by all the girls.

The day came when Malini stood alone. Later she took a step. This, however, proved to be a problem because she had a great fear of falling. Everyone helped by making a joke out of each fall. At last the battle was won. A fall did not mean a thing except providing for her another chance to laugh.

Because of God's loving touch upon her, sad little Malini became a garland of joy, entwining herself around the hearts of all the Honeysuckle Family and the whole of the Mukti Mission, too.

As she began to grow, I would often slip into the prayer time and see Malini sitting in Ruth Akka's lap. She took her turn to pray, repeating each word carefully in a sweet, high-pitched voice after her Akka. The others were still praying for her. These are some of the things they said.

"Thank you, Lord Jesus, for bringing Malini to us," began one of them.

"Thank you for making her laugh," said another.

"Thank you for strengthening her legs and back so that she can walk," added another.

Malini grew to be an apparently healthy young teenager. But then an emergency arose. She began to experience excruciating kidney pains and was taken to a Christian hospital about 100 miles from us. There, Dr. A. Ranbhese, a dear friend of my Honeysuckle Family, and other doctors, discovered that this kidney pain was caused by a delayed defect in her kidney cells that had broken out into a major infection. They felt it was as a result of her childhood malnutrition and began to treat it. Dr. Ranbhese informed me that she was not responding to the medication and suggested that I postpone my upcoming furlough in case her illness should prove to be fatal.

The doctor informed me that there was one new medication they were going to try on her, but he wanted me to be aware that they did not know if it would help. Oh, how we prayed for her recovery.

The phone rang in my office at Mukti. It was a long-distance call from Dr. Ranbhese. "Miss Doerksen, you can go on your furlough. The medication had been successful," he said happily.

Malini returned home and her health improved completely. She loved music and played the violin every Sunday in the church and participated in evangelistic work and was a real blessing to us all. When an opportunity came for marriage, I was happy to recommend her and she responded to my choice. Soon we were getting ready for a lovely wedding. She and her husband are now involved in a church and ministry in a city about 100 miles from Mukti and have a son and daughter who are doing well in school.

CHRISTMAS HAPPINESS

Just before Christmas 1965, Tara became a little comet of happiness to reflect the light of Him who became the Light of the world. In family prayers one evening, Ruth Akka told the story of a little girl also named Tara, who had led her brother to the Savior through her prayers and faithful witness. It was at a Christmas program, where this Tara had taken her brother that her prayer was answered. That evening, after family prayers our Tara was very serious and her eyes glistened with tears.

"My name is Tara, too," she said, "but I could not lead anyone to Jesus, because I have never received Him myself." As He became her own Savior, Tara's eyes shone with happiness. She began to pray that night for her Honeysuckle sisters, who as yet had not made room in their hearts for the Lord Jesus, and also for her Hindu classmates.

Tara was thrilled when eight months later her prayers were answered and Nilprabha (Blue Dawn) had a wonderful experience. While reading her Bible in a quiet corner one evening, she felt the Lord Jesus speaking to her heart. She came to tell me that God had spoken to her and showed her that she must share the story of the Savior's love with Nilprabha.

Honeysuckle Family with Anne Siemens from Canada in Clothes that Came in the Drums from Canada

Dr. Dhekney, Principal of Commerce College, Pune University, Came to Celebrate Jesus' Birthday—Christmas Morning

"How can you share the message of one whom you have not received as your own Savior?" I asked. The Holy Spirit had prepared her heart and how happy she was when we got up from our knees that evening. She was ready to tell others of His love, for now she understood it.

Some weeks later Suwerna, who is also Nilprabha's classmate, started to cry at family prayers, during the singing of the hymn, "Behold I am standing at the door of your heart and knocking." She asked the Savior to come into her heart and cleanse her. "Dear Lord," she wept, "I'm an awful sinner. I stole the sweets [candy] from the cupboard. No one else in the family seems to steal, but I've done it again and again. Can you forgive me, and come into my heart and cleanse me?" He did just this, and we have bowed in thanks and praise, over and over again, at

Dr. Dhekney on Our Walk with the Honeysuckle Family at Christmas with the Girls of our Honeysuckle Family Wearing Dresses Sewn by Ladies' Missionary Society of Lillian's Church

the sweet change and joy that we saw in our "Good Fold," which is what her last name means. My Honeysuckle Wonders had become just that!

My three sisters—Rosella and her husband, Walter; Mabel and her husband, George; and Viola and her husband, Harold—have all been to India to visit me and see the ministry there. How they enjoyed our Honeysuckle

Family. The girls loved them and considered them their real aunties and uncles. Walter, who was a carpenter, built a lovely cupboard and fixed a large stainless steel sink in it, on our verandah. The girls adored him for this. They would wash their hands, faces and hair in the sink instead of getting all wet under the low tap outside. We were the only family that had a sink; it was useful in so many ways.

Chapter Seven

&

THE WAGON
OF LIGHT

Transportation by bullock cart was always slow and tortuous. It didn't seem possible that we would ever have anything better to get around in the villages for our evangelistic camps. However, a miracle took place during a visit to Southern California during my 1964 furlough.

I was meeting with Torchy Lapic, a lovely red-haired lady who had heard about Mukti at a ladies' prayer meeting when I was at BIOLA in Los Angeles. The owner of a pharmacy store in Ojai, California, she had been supporting Anjali, one of my girls. As we talked in her home, I shared with Torchy some of the wonderful things God was doing in Anjali's life as well as in the other girls in Mukti. She was so impressed that she not only took me to town to buy a lot of clothes and other surprises to take back to the girls in my family, but she also offered to take me out for dinner.

"Where would you like to go, Lillian?" she asked. I smiled and then replied, "Well, Torchy, we passed an interesting looking place on our way to the shops. Why don't we go there?" A smile crossed her face as she drove us there in her beautiful Daimler. "Lillian, you may have wondered why I smiled when you suggested this place," she said as we were shown to our table. "Well, the reason is that I love car racing and you can see on all of the shelves of the restaurant here are miniature racing cars." Torchy was certainly an unusual pharmacist. Her vivacious personality made her so much fun to be with. Over our meal she kept firing questions at me about the work in India.

After dinner, she took me back to her shiny black Daimler. "It's all I've got now," she sighed as she put the key in the ignition and the engine purred into life. I laughed as this was the kind of car that the prime minister of India would use. I knew she had owned an incredible array of glamorous sports cars. Torchy drove me around a lovely community outside Ojai while I felt like royalty.

When we came to a halt at a stoplight, I saw a van pull up alongside us. I had been telling her about the evangelistic camps we had in Mukti where we went to the villages, lived in tents and visited the villagers in a bullock cart to give out the gospel. "That's a Volkswagen van," she said. "That one is a basic model, Lillian, but there are some that are equipped with everything. You could sleep in it and some even have fridges. Wouldn't one of those be great to have in the camps for your villages?" she asked.

"Wouldn't that be great," I echoed, knowing we couldn't even dream of such a thing.

The next day I jumped as the telephone shrilled at 7:00 A.M. It was Good Friday and I was getting ready to leave after breakfast for Fresno. I had been staying for several months at the home of Ralph and Bernie Kemprud in Glendale, so I could take a writer's course at a Los Angeles university. The Kempruds had moved from Vancouver to Glendale, California.

"It's for you," said Ralph, as he handed me the receiver. It was Torchy, who asked me on the phone to postpone my going because she said she had hardly slept that night. I asked if she was worried about her father, who was sick. "No, no," she answered, "God was not letting me sleep. He has shown me very clearly to get you a Volkswagen van for you to take back to India. He wants me to have the joy of helping my neighbors in India and to share in your vital ministry of caring for the needy children there."

Torchy seemed to read my mind that was questioning why she wanted to do this. "Lil," she explained, "you know that I have been ill, but God has wonderfully raised me up to health. I have great joy in being able to serve Him in this way." I was totally speechless. Then I told her about the problems of getting the vehicle into India and the high duty that could be involved. "Look Lil, God has already done two miracles this morning, will you pray with me that He will work one more?" she asked.

I agreed to pray, but I needed to know about these miracles. She told me that she had phoned her car dealer at 5:00 A.M. and he had said that they had in stock a 1964 Volkswagen Station Wagon van that had only 6,000 miles on the clock. He said it was for sale, available immediately and in perfect shape. "Then, at six o'clock this morning, I woke up my banker and told him that I needed an immediate loan on my house this morning. He said he would go down to the bank and see what he could do for me. He said to me, 'Torchy, I know that if God shows you something, it will have to be done. You are fantastic with your faith in God. Come and see me at eight o'clock at the bank.'"

What could I do? I had to promise her to pray, but I knew that it was impossible. I told her to hold off with the purchase until I called her back, because at nine o'clock I would call the high commissioner for India in the San Francisco office to ask about a permit to get it into India.

"Torchy, don't do anything until I talk to him," I said.

When I phoned, I managed to get the high commissioner on the line. "Madam, if you have lived in India, you know as well as I do, it's hardly possible to take a car to India," he told me in an abrupt manner. So I told him over the phone the unusual story of my phone call from Torchy. Then I shared that I was from Ramabai Mukti Mission, and he asked curtly, "What is it?"

I patiently explained about the work. He listened quietly and said he had heard about Pandita Ramabai but had not heard about the mission and he was interested to hear all about it. I told him that I had to leave that day, and would be in Fresno for Easter Sunday. I gave him the address where I would be staying. He told me that even though it was Good Friday, he would immediately send a staff worker with the documents for me to complete for the importation of the vehicle.

"He will take them to the San Francisco airport and give the packet to the pilot going to Sacramento," he explained. "He, in turn, will give it to the pilot of the Fresno plane that leaves in the afternoon and you should receive it the same day.

"Be sure to fill the forms out immediately and then send them by special airmail delivery to the chief controller of imports and exports at the Ministry of Commerce and Industry in New Delhi," he ordered. He knew that I had to leave for India in a short time and wanted me to have the permit in hand before I left, so I could take the Volkswagen van on the ship with me. He emphasized that I should get the documents off the next day, Saturday morning, "for sure."

When I phoned Torchy back and told her about his message, she was thrilled and said, "Lillian, just stay there 'til I come. Don't go anywhere."

I phoned my sister Orlean, in Fresno and told her that I would not be there for lunch as I had promised. When she heard why, she was all excited. To me, it just seemed like a big dream that I was supposed to be getting a van that day. I told her that she would see me when she saw me. At two in the afternoon the doorbell rang, and there was Torchy with a big smile. "Get the bottle—the bottle of milk I mean—and come out and let's christen the van," she said excitedly.

I went down the steps and when I saw the beautiful red, shiny Volkswagen van with the new license plate on it and the registration papers all made out in my name, I could hardly believe it. "We don't need milk, Torchy," I said. "I can christen it with my tears." We joyfully thanked the Lord and I nicknamed it "The Wonder Wagon," although others called it "The Buds and Blossoms Buggy" and also "The Wagon of Light."

As I traveled in North America I had been doing some radio interviews about the ministry. Shortly after one of them, I received a phone call at the Kemprud's and a man on the other end of the line said he had heard me speak on the radio. "I need you to stop by my home," he insisted. Much against my better judgment, I did so. This unusual listener explained that God had appointed him as a latter-day prophet. Then, this most eccentric man told me to take his message to India. I told him I couldn't do that for I had to be loyal to the Ramabai Mukti Mission and I told him all about it. Then he wanted to go with me to a bank that was on the way to the freeway taking me north. He hopped in the van with me and I prayed hard that nothing bad would happen to me.

When we arrived at his bank, he could see that I was getting edgy and made me promise that I would not leave until he came back. Because it was such a strange situation, I was anxious to just take off. I was about to leave when he eventually emerged from the bank, opened the passenger door and slid in beside me. Then he grabbed my purse, but instead of taking something out of it, he started putting something in it. I did not know how much it was, but I saw it was a lot of bills. I thanked him and said it would come in handy to help ship the new van. I then asked if we could have a word of prayer to thank God. "No," he said curtly, "I only pray in the dark." And with that he opened the door of the van and was gone. I shook my head in disbelief and sped off, driving north towards my next stop in my new Wagon of Light.

I knew that I would probably have a problem getting the vehicle over the border into Canada, from where I planned to ship it to India. From Fresno, I had phoned and hastily written an express letter to the Canadian border authorities at Sumas, Washington, explaining everything that had happened and giving them the phone number of my friend in Everett, Washington, where I planned to stop off. I requested that they kindly grant me a permit to bring it into Canada and use it there until it was shipped.

After a happy Easter with my sister Orlean and her family in Fresno I left for Washington State. When I called my friends in Everett from Seattle, I was told there was a message waiting for me. The phone had rung and they had been asked to take a collect call from the Canadian customs office at the border. "Please tell Miss Lillian Doerksen, who will be passing through there either today or tomorrow, that her permit for the Volkswagen will be waiting for her at the border."

I stopped by the office of my friend Viola Dand in Seattle and told the whole miracle story to her. As I sat by her desk and recounted all of the astonishing things that had already taken place, including the story of the "prophet" who had taken me to his bank, her boss who had been quietly listening to everything in an adjoining room, suddenly walked over to me.

"I heard your story and I wondered how much that fellow actually gave you?" he asked.

I felt my face flush with embarrassment. "Do you know, I never checked." With that, I opened my purse and began pulling out the bills and we counted them. There was a total of $600! I was floored. What amazing things our God does!

Touch a Miracle

When I arrived at the border the following day, I parked the van and walked into the customs office there. There I noticed my letter and a prayer card that I had attached with it on a table. Lying beside it was the permit. Things were quiet at the border and so I was able to share with the officers about what I was doing in India. I also had an opportunity to witness to them. After this they said they wanted to see the miracle van. So I asked them to come outside and "touch a miracle." They did—and they did not open a door or want to examine the things that had been given to me for the children of India. The van was loaded with all kinds of materials that had been given me. On a previous visit to the States, when a women's group had given me a lot of dresses for my girls, I had had to leave my car full at the border overnight. The next day my father came and we did a lot of praying and talking to get the dresses over. I could hardly believe what was happening now.

I sailed off in the Volkswagen with a light heart, full of wonder and praise for God's wonderful doings. I visited the Indian trade commissioner in Vancouver, and he was also interested in my story and immediately sent messages to New Delhi to try to help me get a permit to get it into India. However, it did not arrive in time to take the van with me. I sailed again for India, without my beloved Wagon of Light.

I was in New Delhi, India's capital city to try to see Dr. S. Radhakrishnan, the president of India, in a bid to enlist his help in getting an import permit for the vehicle. I had visited his secretary at Rashtrapati Bhavan, the president's ceremonial residence, and tried to explain why I needed to see the leader. "The President," he informed me, "is very busy with appointments all day and all evening. In fact, he is booked solid for two weeks." The secretary added that he did not think I had a chance of seeing him. After I told him of my mission and gave him a copy of Pandita Ramabai's *A Testimony*, he promised to do his best.

When I got back to the YWCA where I was staying, the manager said that I had received a call from the president's office saying that the president wanted to see me at 9:30 A.M. I did not get a wink of sleep that June night in 1965. The humidity was so intense that I felt I was inside a sauna. In the morning, however, a wall of gray mist came in and the rain broke, bringing some relief. I took a taxi to Rashtrapati Bhavan, and arrived half an hour early. As the taxi entered the gates, the guards saluted, and one asked, "Miss Lillian?" I nodded and he waved me on from one gate to the next. When I arrived at the Bhavan, I was received with dignity by the president's aides who were waiting for me. I smiled my way along as they took me past guards posted every few feet, nodding at each as they saluted. In the reception rooms it was the same. One promptly brought a tray with coffee, cookies and water; another brought the morning papers and a third came around offering me cigarettes.

I refused these, of course, but was happy to listen when the secretary coached me on protocol. He made it very clear that I was being given ten minutes of the chief minister of our state's time and that I must be sure to finish my presentation in those ten minutes.

I waved formalities aside, as other aides made an attempt at friendly conversation, and shared with them about Pandita Ramabai and her testimony. They were soon so interested in hearing about Mukti and asking questions that the half hour was gone before we knew it. Then the president rang for me to be presented to him. The words of the aide thrilled me as he bowed low and said, "The president wishes to see you. He asked you to come now."

I had expected to be formally ushered into one of the magnificent receiving rooms, but instead when the door opened there I was in the homiest "bedroom." The president was reclining on his bed, relaxed and with books, papers and everything around him. He was so friendly and informal that I felt almost as though I was visiting an important uncle. He ordered tea for me, and it was beautifully but simply served with biscuits (cookies) and cashew nuts. I knew that interviews were seldom more than fifteen minutes long, but he urged me to have tea.

"Miss Doerksen, why are you in India?" he asked.

That gave me an opportunity to tell him what it meant to know Christ, and of His call on my life. He seemed very interested in Mukti and asked a number of questions. I gave him an invitation to visit us. Then he posed an interesting question to me. "Why," he asked, "did Pandita Ramabai become a Christian?"

I looked at him for a moment and then responded, "Sir, she can tell you better than I can." The president looked at me with a questioning look, so I handed him a copy of the book Pandita Ramabai called simply, *A Testimony*. He received it eagerly from me and then asked his aide to bring me another cup of tea. He said he knew about Ramabai but was so glad to have something written by her. As he did, he excitedly leafed through the book and then turning his gaze on me said, "Now Miss Doerksen, what can I do for you?" Imagine—this was the president of India! I had to pinch myself that I was in his presence. He was so easy to talk to. Then I realized that twenty minutes had already slipped by, and that I had better get on with the purpose of my visit. I told him the story of the Volkswagen and gave him my three-fold request to consider. I asked for a permit for the wagon to be imported, a permit for the necessary parts to be imported and finally, requested exemption of duty on the van.

He seemed interested when I told him how I hoped the van could be used to take children outside of the four walls for picnics, retreats and medical attention. I also shared with him my burden for the Mukti workers and leaders to be able get away on retreats with their orphan families. He told one of his aides to get all of the information from me and then wished me well in our work.

In return I wished him God's blessing and assured him of our prayers. I left him still clutching Ramabai's testimony.

When I was taken to the reception office again, I was seated beside a gentleman who was waiting to see the president. We shook hands and were introduced. He was Mr. Naik, the chief minister of Maharashtra. I was so surprised and he asked me who I was. I was glad to briefly tell him about the work and leave a prayer card with him. I knew I had been given a slice of his time with the president. I also apologized for taking more of his time and invited him to come and visit us. He said he would like to if we had an important enough occasion. He went into the president's presence with my prayer card in his hand.

After a visit with the family who had originally invited me to come to see the president, and a great opportunity of sharing the message of God's love and life in Christ with them, I flew by plane to Bombay and then took the train home. On the train as I meditated on those three days of interesting and eventful opportunities for Christ, my heart seemed to join the rhythm of the wheels as the train sped along, taking me back to Mukti to share all these wonderful things and to take up the duties and joys that awaited me there.

A verse that God blessed to my heart in those days was Philippians 1:21, "For me living means opportunities for Christ" (LB).

When I went to the post box some days later, I was surprised to see an official letter from the president of India. I tore it open and got the good news saying that the permit to import the vehicle was granted.

It was wonderful to see that donations for the import duty had come in from Indian co-workers and friends. When the vehicle arrived and I went into the customs office at Bombay, I wondered if the donations that I had been given would be enough to cover the import duty. You can imagine my surprise when I was told that the import duty had been reduced to just 80 percent (I had been told that it had been 200 and then 180 percent the previous year). When I discussed the amount I would have to pay with an officer, he reduced the quoted price of the vehicle by taking off eight months' depreciation. Then I asked him, "Sir, is it right to pay duty on a duty that has already been paid?"

"Of course not," he replied.

I reminded him that it was a German vehicle that had been imported into the US, where duty had been paid. So the sale price of the vehicle included this duty. He went to the shelf and took out a Volkswagen catalogue from Germany and finally came to the decision that it would only be 5,790 rupees, which at that time was about eight rupees to the US dollar.

My heart jumped, for gifts that had been given amounted to over 7,000 rupees, which meant we would have money to fix up a garage for the van.

The Wagon of Light had finally arrived in India! What a celebration there was when I pulled up at the front gate of Mukti in this shiny red van that was going to be such a blessing to our work.

A DOUBLE MIRACLE

Sulochina Tai ("Sulitai", as we lovingly called her) became our matron-mother after Ruth Akka was married. She, and her husband Vasant, who was the caretaker at our school, lived just across the street from us. They usually joined us in family parties, Saturday night family prayer times and also often on trips and outings in our Wagon of Light.

After several years, during which they had had no children of their own, Sulitai came to wish me a "happy birthday." I met her at the front gate where I was getting information on and photographing a little baby left at our front gate. She came over just as the superintendent, Rohini Gadre came to do the interview and see to the admission of the baby. Sulitai asked the superintendent, "Which family will you place the baby in? Do you give babies like this in adoption? We have been praying about adopting a baby, since we cannot seem to have our own child."

That afternoon when Sulitai and Vasant came over for my birthday party, we were surprised when the superinten-

Dedication of Sulitai and Vasant's Baby Rani (Princess) in Mukti Church. Honeysuckles in Front Two Rows

dent came to the door with a baby in her arms. She came in and handed the sweet little one into Sulitai's arms. "The committee met and has agreed to give you this baby for adoption. She's yours," she said. What an exciting party it turned out to be!

How we all loved little Rani! What a surprise we had when, some months later, Sulitai found out that she was pregnant. They had a lovely son. What a happy family!

We joined in the happy Sunday a few months later when she was dedicated in our Mukti church and named Prerana. However, we all loved her and called her Rani for she was our little princess. Rani grew up to be a much-loved nurse after training in the big Christian hospital in Miraj.

Chapter Eight

Preparing for Leadership

I could tell by the grimace on his face that the man I had come to see was not happy. He was the education minister for Maharashtra State and I had traveled to Bombay to try to persuade him to help us. Because it was now 1:30 P.M., he obviously wanted to leave the secretariat building where he was based and partake of a hearty and spicy lunch in a nearby restaurant, and here I was preventing that.

It was well past his normal mealtime, and he was running late with appointments in his Bombay office. I had been waiting in the lobby for several hours. I knew that I needed to acquire a thick skin for a few brief moments to get his attention, or we would have no high school in Kedgaon. The future was at stake. We needed a girls' high school for which I had sent him an application.

It would have been easy for us as missionaries to have continued the status quo for as long as possible. I felt that it was vitally important for us to prepare our girls to be national leaders, so they could continue the work for Christ in India long after we had left, or the doors had closed to western missionary work.

Lillian, Publicity Office Training National Leaders: Nalini, Dorothy, and Lydia

There had been twenty-eight missionaries on the staff when I arrived, and one by one they had retired. It was clear to me that our prime role should be to prepare our girls to become leaders in our places. We saw that this was a vision from God. There is only one missionary now left and she is overdue for her retirement.

The standard of education was improving in our primary school, and the educational authorities were impressed. The numbers, too, were growing. The problem was that when they got their final certificates at seventh grade, it was difficult to find admission to a good Christian, boarding high school. They needed high school in order to go to college and Bible school, so they could train to become leaders. So the urgency of a high school in Kedgoan became one of my great goals, even though I had

Central Publicity Manager (Training National Leaders)

a heavy schedule of responsibility, including managing the Publicity Department, the printing press, training young girls in printing and my Honeysuckle Family of orphan girls who were a major involvement in my life.

A Wall of Difficulties

We faced a wall of difficulties regarding our high school—the major one being obtaining the permission of our Indian Ramabai Mukti Mission board, which was made up of missionaries and several Indian staff members, to build the high school. The board maintained that they were not in a good enough financial situation to consider such a big project. Because of my complete assurance that this was God's will, I kept praying and I also kept the board members aware of the need of the high school. My visits with

Sharada Sadan School, Principal Lillian

the education authorities in Poona resulted in their assurance, that with their help, we would get the proper permits from the ministry of education for permission to begin a high school for girls.

They had helped to get an appointment for me to visit the state's minister of education in Bombay. I had traveled all night in a second-class compartment so crowded I couldn't even cross my legs. I arrived in the morning to find the minister was busy for a couple of hours. I phoned a Christian Indian friend of mine, Jhinny Bilimoria, and she came with me. We sat in the lobby of the secretariat and talked and prayed for several hours. Then, finally, I was called into the minister's office.

It was now ninety minutes after the normal lunch time, and most people had left for their lunch. The minister, how-

Principal Lillian with Teachers of Mukti School

ever, was still in his office. Two of his friends were standing by his door apparently ready to go for lunch with him. What a time to expect to get a hearing for this important business! He hurriedly asked me, "What is it that you want?"

I told him that he had heard about our need in Kedgaon to start a girl's high school. He frowned and I remembered that I had heard that he was more interested in starting co-ed schools in the state. He answered harshly, "Oh yes, that's in competition with the school that is being initiated by one of our parliament members."

"Sir, we are not interested in any competition," I answered quickly. "I feel we have a legitimate need for our girl's high school. In the villages, parents are not willing to send their girls to a high school where there are mostly boys. There is a real need for a girl's high school. Fathers come to me to take girls that are only eleven and twelve years of age out of school to be married. Not only that, but you know that Mararashtra State stands first in its family planning program in our country. Sir, can't you see what a girl's high school would do in our family planning program?"

He looked at me and I could tell he thought that what I had said was stupid. He turned to his desk and sat down, so I was able to sit down, too, across from him.

"What do you mean?" he said.

"Sir, do you know that I have made a survey of the schools in our district and I find that up to fourth grade,

Deputy Director of Education Mr. Awale, Rajas Dongre, Lillian, and Vimal Dongte at Dedication Ceremony and Unveiling of Cornerstone of Manorama Memorial Girls' High School

there is almost an equal number of boys and girls in school. But when they reach the seventh standard and have to write the final government exam, the most girls I found in that class were four. Can't you see what this is doing to our family planning plan?"

The minister held up his hand interrupting me and asked if I did not know that he was the minister of education and was aware of the situation in the state. "Miss

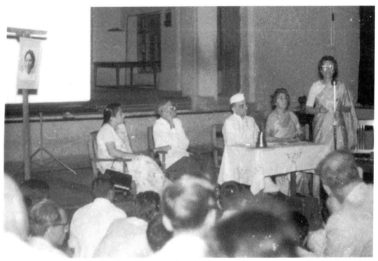

Lillian, Principal of New High School

Doerksen," he said, "we have received ninety other applications to begin girl's high schools, which I am not considering, because I still believe firmly that we need co-ed schools."

"But," I countered, "if girls could stay in school for another four years of high school and possibly go on to college and marriages were delayed, what a boost this would be to family planning. And, besides, think of how girls with more education could benefit the uplift of life in the villages."

In a softer tone this time, the minister said, "I'll think about it."

I looked at him and said, "Thank you. That's all I ask—that you think about it, sir!"

With that he hurried off for lunch and I returned to Mukti and informed the local educational authorities of the result of my visit. It was just two weeks later that the official permission to build our high school came through. With this in hand, I asked the Mukti board to again consider supporting the project. To strengthen my hand, members of the local educational authorities in Pune decided they would come and meet the board and emphasize the importance of my request. Just before they arrived, there was a telegram from the New Zealand Mukti board, with the surprising message that they were sending five hundred pounds for the building of a high school. With this encouragement, the board passed the required motion. It was not necessary for the local education authorities to visit them to persuade them further.

With this breakthrough, I was hardly prepared for all the other difficulties that stood before me. One was the need for workers to build the foundation before our annual school homecoming for graduated students. The railway was engaged in a major construction project that had claimed workers from our mission as well as men from all around. Where would we get the craftsmen to get the foundation ready? We prayed, and the day before the meeting, the railway project was completed and there was a whole team of workers ready to lay the foundation. They worked all night and the next day as our meeting proceeded.

There were two other major problems. Steel for the structure was hard to procure and cement was almost impossible to get for such a building project. I assumed that it was because so much new building was going on in the country and that this had caused a major shortage. We had been able to obtain six bags, which was the maximum for an agricultural project that we had, but nothing for construction. How we needed a miracle from God! But would it happen?

Dr. Dhekney, a dear friend and the principal of the commerce college of Pune University, was extremely interested in our high school project. He accompanied me to Bombay and introduced me to many important people in government to share about the ministry we had. He even invited me to come to Bombay with him to meet some friends he thought might help me.

When we arrived in Bombay, he asked me to stop in with him at the office of one of his past students. Dr. Dhekney was greatly revered by his students. We got to the office where we exchanged a few humorous remarks and I was ready to go on to meet the next official. He was a former student, too. As I shared with him about the work of Mukti, the project on my heart, and the need for cement, he pricked up his ears and I saw an expression come on his face that surprised me. He informed me while we were in the office that his was a great cement company and that all the cement we needed would be supplied in a week.

One day we were informed by the station master that a railway car had just been pulled onto a side track of our Kedgaon station. It was a railroad car filled with cement for us! It had taken two weeks. How could we thank God enough for His great and loving ways?

I personally had to oversee much of the supervision of the workers and many of the purchases of products needed. They also said obtaining steel was impossible. I visited a steel factory where the manager was very kind. He listened to my story and the great need for our girl's high school and of my dedication to meet the needs of orphan and village girls. Though it was difficult, he was able to provide all the steel that was needed for the beams and structure of the building.

Mrs. Laxshmi Menon, minister of external affairs, was our special guest at the groundbreaking ceremony to turn the sod for the high school to be built. When the new structure of the high school was finally up, there was a dedication service and it was dedicated to the memory of Bhimabai, who had been the much-loved headmistress of the primary school before I came there.

A concern of mine was the training of our own girls who had already had college. I was able to encourage and help them to go to seminary and for other training to prepare them for staff leadership. Vimalbai Dongre, who was a teacher on the staff, replaced me as the principal after a year of extra training in the USA. The school has grown and how grateful we were for all the rewards in the lives of the young people who are in leadership and are making a contribution to their communities and Mukti. Among them are Kamal Deshpande and Rohini Gadre, who were able to go to seminary and also became leaders in Mukti. Many others also became effective workers on the staff. Others are guardians, matrons of the large orphan families, the handicapped, blind and elderly, evangelists in the villages and other staff workers.

Each year, we held our Founder's Day Celebration on March 11. We were excited that on the day that we were to have our dedication for the foundation-laying event, the main speaker was Tarabai McKenzie, who grew up in Mukti. She had been a teacher on the staff, and was now a home-maker and leader in Sholapur, the community in which she lived.

She told all the children and the staff, after making a generous gift to the mission, "It is always a joy to come home to Mukti and see something new that God has done. We praise God for all that He has done. Because the training of our young people is so important, we praise God with all of our hearts for what He is doing to make it possible for this project of the assembly hall and high school to be erected. God who has supplied the needs through the years will provide every need for this, too.

"It is because of all the wonderful training that I have received here in Mukti that I have success in my life now. When I was here, I learned among other things that 'it is more blessed to give than to receive.' I have, with others, received education and training here that has blessed my life, and now, it is our responsibility to give ourselves to God to help others. I learned, too, that the fear of God is the beginning of wisdom." The donations from the former students and parents that day amounted to the generous amount of one thousand rupees, which was received with special thanksgiving.

There are over 1,000 girls in the school now.

Chapter Nine

❧

Don't Wrestle, Just Nestle

There were wonderful joys in caring for and training a large family of girls, as well as serving the Lord in many other areas—as principal of our large school, manager of the publicity office with its many demands, training girls in the printing press and many other demanding responsibilities there.

We saw God work not only in the lives of our girls, but also in the hearts of the Hindu boys and girls from the villages, in the school and village Sunday school outreaches. All of the different ministries had been very rewarding, but meant leaning on the Lord who had called me so I would be able to fulfill all of the demands on my time and strength.

So many times when I thought of the little scraps of humanity left at the mission, who now gave us and the Savior so much joy, I have been challenged by the memory of Ramabai, that great scholar and saint of God in India through whom He founded Mukti, this Home of Salvation.

God had promised Ramabai that from those many thousands who should find refuge and salvation there, He would form a cornerstone for the church of Christ in India.

From Psalm 144:12, He promised her, "That our sons may be as plants, grown up in their youth; that our daughters may be as corner stones, polished after the similitude of a palace."

Inside the large, beautiful stone church at Mukti that seats over 2,000 (the largest Christian place of worship in western India at that time), she placed this verse as a reminder of His faithfulness. It was on the wall of the church for all to see and remember.

On top of all my responsibilities, I was asked to be the hostess for visitors who came through to see Mukti almost every day, and to entertain even chief ministers and other high government officials. I wondered if I would be able to carry this task out, as well. I found it becoming increasingly difficult to face unexpected situations in my large family with all the other duties and demands on my time and energy.

I was becoming tired beyond words—and so began a walk through a valley of darkness.

It was pressure, pressure, pressure. Like the unexpected extra responsibility of helping Satejela, one of my miracle children who now needed immediate medical attention and possible heart surgery. Because of this, I had to leave Mukti for the hills to collect her from the boarding school where she was studying. This was a four-hour trip. Then I had to take her to the Wanless Hospital, a Christian facility in Miraj, another six hours by train.

Satejela, who had been very active in sports and in music, was devastated when it was discovered during a routine medical examination that she had a hole in her heart. She was told she could not play sports any more and she had become very depressed about the situation.

As we sat together in the train carriage, I tried to comfort her, but she cried for she kept thinking about her future and was too afraid to face it.

At the hospital, I asked the doctor exactly what was going to happen and who was going to operate. After he had examined her, he said the operation would be on the following Monday. When she heard the word *operation* she burst into tears and could not control herself. The thought of her body being cut open haunted her as she slept. On Monday morning she woke up at 3:00 A.M. and prayed for the Lord to give her courage to face that day.

He gave her the verse He had given her earlier: Isaiah 41:10, "Fear thou not for I am with thee. Be not dismayed for I am thy God; I will strengthen thee; yea I will help thee; yea I will uphold thee with the right hand of my righteousness."

When she received that verse, she felt God's peace coming into her heart and was happy and comforted. She knew many dear ones were in prayer for her. She was no longer scared of the operation, but still had an awful fear of injections because she had so many when she was little.

Like so many of our children, Satejela had been another castaway. I remember the day that she came. I was called to the Mukti gate where I was told a new baby had arrived. I grabbed my camera and hurried there to meet a woman and a young girl, hardly twelve years old, who was the mother of the tiny baby that was lying on a cot in our admission room. The woman, who was the young mother's aunt, told me that that the child was thirteen months old, which seemed impossible. The baby was just skin and bone, and when we weighed her was less than ten pounds.

As the woman handed over the child, she explained that she belonged to her young niece. She was caring for the niece after her mother and father had died. Lapsing into coarse language, she told us bitterly that the man who tended the bullocks had raped this young girl and disgraced her family.

"You don't have to show your anger in this way," I said. "We will take the baby because we know that the girl cannot take care of her," I said.

I discovered that she and the girl had been trying to starve the baby, hoping that it would die. There was a Christian school nearby that this girl had attended and they told the aunt about our mission and told her to take the baby here.

We accepted the child and I volunteered to take her into our Honeysuckle Family, even though I was aware that I could hardly find the time that I knew I needed to give her.

That evening at our family prayer time, everyone was gathered around Ruth Akka, who had the child on her knee. "We are trying to choose a name for our new baby," Ruth Akka said.

"What do you want to call her?" I asked the children.

Just then I was called away by the superintendent, and Ruth Akka led the prayers. When I came back they were still sitting on the floor and they told me happily that they had chosen a name for her.

"What is it?" I asked.

Ruth Akka replied, "We were reading in Hebrews, chapter four and verse twelve, and we saw a word that caught our attention. In verse twelve it says that 'God's Word is *satej*, which means "quicker than light" in our language. Couldn't we call her *Satejbala*? (Quicker-than-light baby)?"

"Wouldn't that be a great name for her?" Suhasani asked excitedly.

I was so pleased. That sweet little baby who looked like a two-month-old, became our treasure. With good food and Ruth Akka's daily massage, and naps in the sun, she soon became a normal, happy baby. She went to our kindergarten and then I was able to send her to Kimmins, an excellent English medium Christian boarding school away in the hills with her Honeysuckle sisters, Anjali and Jayabala.

Satej was a bright girl and at the boarding school she not only excelled in studies and sports, which she loved, but also in music and in Christian leadership.

She was always a very sensitive child. Because she had had so many injections when she was a baby to help her gain health and strength, she was afraid of them. I thanked God for the wonderful things He had done in her life. As I prayed for her courage and strength for the surgery, I was so happy to know that she found strength from God's Word, too. I claimed the promise with her, and gave her another in Psalm 73:26, "God is the strength of my heart and my portion forever."

The day of the operation I stood with a group of medical college students on the second floor looking through the glass ceiling. Seeing Dr. J. Thomas, the cardiologist, praying before the operation helped me feel God's soothing presence.

I watched as they brought this already anesthetized fourteen-year-old into the operating room. With great earnestness, I asked the Lord to direct the surgeon's hands. I felt my jaw tighten as I observed this skilled man use the scalpel to make a deep incision. He opened up her chest and revealed the beating heart with a hole in it. I continued to watch as he stitched a nylon patch onto that hole and then sewed her up again.

Later, when Satej regained consciousness in her room, she was covered with many tubes and needles. The following day when Dr. Sheik, a non-Christian doctor, came to remove the tubes she started to cry, for she thought it meant another injection. He explained gently that he would very carefully remove the tubes. She asked him to call me.

He told her I would not be able to come to her side and then began removing the tubes. Just then I walked through the door of the intensive care room. Her tears quickly disappeared when she saw me. But when he started to remove those tubes, she again began to cry. "I can't bear it! Stop!" she called out in great pain.

The doctor stopped and looked in my direction. I walked over to the bed and whispered in her ear, "Satej, say this instead, 'I *can* bear it. Lord help me!'" She repeated these words over and over, and the Lord helped her to bear the pain as the doctor again began removing the tubes.

The doctor was impressed with her prayer and she later had the privilege of sharing with him about the Savior. She recovered quickly and desired with all her heart to do His will, because He had been so gracious to her. She has never had any heart trouble since then.

As I could see she was making a good recovery, I hurried back to Mukti, for demanding deadlines in the publicity office and other responsibilities were urgent. I was eventually able to rush back to the hospital and was so thrilled to see her amazing recovery. We had a great time of sharing as we traveled back.

Later, Satej wanted to have one year of Bible college in Bangalore in thanksgiving and praise for what God had done for her. At the Bible college, she helped in a Christian deaf school that a deaf missionary who was a professor at the Bible college had started. There she met Rama, a fine young student in the college, who had remembered seeing her at the Bible college. He came to visit his deaf professor where she worked. She wrote to me about him and asked if I would grant his request to correspond with her. I answered, "No, not until I have met him." Soon after that I went to Bombay to meet him as he was working for a Christian organization there. I was pleased with him and so they began to correspond with each other.

He then became a pastor. I was very ready to consent to their engagement when they felt God had already planned it!

As with my other girls, I made investigations and got references from those who knew him. I checked on how he was going to support her and where they were going to live. I then gave all this information to the superintendent of Mukti and the marriage committee that is made up of the pastor of the local church, and members of the Mukti staff.

The couple, if approved, is then allowed to meet. If after a short meeting the two emerge smiling, we know it has "clicked." Religious, economic, home conditions and education have all been checked. It is just their personalities and their looks that is left for them to work out. If there is any question in the man's mind about the suitability of the girl, he is immediately told to go elsewhere to find a wife. It would not be good psychologically in Mukti for one to be refused and another to be accepted.

However, if the girl feels she is not satisfied with the choice, she will get another opportunity when another offer comes. If the two agree on their suitability, an engagement is arranged. Several weeks later, the bridegroom and his family or pastor, arrive at Mukti, with an engagement sari, blouse, flowers for the bride's hair, bangles (bracelets) for her arms, earrings or an engagement ring. Then the engagement ceremony is performed, followed by a special engagement tea party.

All the girls in her Mukti family and her friends come too, as well as the staff. The date for the wedding is also set at the engagement party.

Our plans worked out very well and we enjoyed a wonderful wedding ceremony in the Mukti chapel.

Satej and Rama have a brilliant little girl called Sarah Lillian and twin boys, Jeevan and Jonathan. Rama is the pastor of the first New Bombay Baptist Church.

Although I was happy with all of these responsibilities in Mukti, the pressure was beginning to weigh me down. There were demands on my strength with the heavy commitments that I had. I did not need the extra fear that sometimes crept in. I honestly felt that God promised abundant strength for those who appropriated it. Yet I did not realize then the demands these stresses were taking on my resources. Weariness led to weakness. When urgent problems arose, it almost culminated in my collapse. I could only praise God that it was not a total collapse.

Nothing in the world is more frightening and crushing than reaching out to God and trying to study His Word and pray and somehow not being able to sense His presence, strength and love in the way you need it.

Satejbala, her precious children and her husband Rama

When Viola Dand, our general secretary for the mission in Canada, came to Mukti, she was shocked when she saw my rundown condition and how completely drained of energy I was.

I explained to her that I just had to get away for at least two months. I did not know where I was going to go. I said, "I know I need one thing, and that is to go somewhere near the sea or mountains where I can just be quiet and somehow see the Lord's greatness and strength again and where I can just be alone with Him."

I did not know this but even before I came home to Vancouver, a friend, Alistair MacKay, who was going to be away for the summer, had offered his beautiful home right on the sea. He was sure that the beauty and quietness of his home was what I needed. His mother, Peggy MacKay, was a very dear friend and had also been for some years the general secretary of our Canadian Mukti board.

The whistle of the Secundrabad Express blew and the train moved slowly away from the platform at Kedgoan. My head moved in Indian assent as loved ones called, "Hurry back! God bless you and bring you back soon." It all seemed so unreal. My heart was strangely torn with love for them all at Mukti, and also with uncertainty. I had been back only a year from furlough, but I was so exhausted that it seemed body, soul and spirit were completely drained of strength. Could it be recovered? Bravely my heart reached out in faith. Would God give His touch and bring me back?

Sinking back in the seat of the train, I felt almost anaesthetized with weakness. Each throb of the engine as it accelerated seemed to synchronize with the throbbing in my head and my aching heart. Each turn of the wheels seemed to tear at my heart with the thought of leaving behind my dear ones in Mukti, especially my loved Honeysuckle Family.

Sulitai, the matron-mother, had just been married and the children seemed to need me more than ever. In order to be together to prepare them for my going away, we had gone for a trip to a lovely hill station for five days. My staff workers, Nalini and Sally, who were to take care of the family, came too. This time meant much to all twenty-five of us, but it had taken almost my last ounce of strength.

Somehow the twenty-eight hour flight from Bombay to New York is almost wiped from my memory. My heart ached with pain trying to sort out what God was trying to show me. I was only in my fifties. Surely my missionary work was not over? I had pleaded with God to help me to appropriate the power which had raised Christ from the dead and that He had promised was available to quicken our mortal bodies. It had only taken an instant to raise Christ from the dead. I had longed for the instant touch of body, soul and spirit, so I would not have to go home. I could not find the answer to that *why?* that tore at my heart. For His special tutoring, God, who writes the scores of our life's melody, knew He needed me apart with the "rest" which foolishly seemed to me to be the end of the tune.

How much it meant to be greeted in New York by Hammond and Julia Major, our US Mukti general secretary and his wife, and my sister Viola, who had flown from Vancouver to meet me at the airport.

Just after my arrival back in Canada, my birthday message on March 17 was Psalm 84:5 and 6. "Happy are those who are strong in the Lord, who want above all else to follow your steps" (LB). Never had I felt more depleted or in need of His strength. The Valley of Weeping was real and I wondered how it could become a place of springs with pools of blessings.

When I walked into the bedroom of the home that Alistair had made available for me and saw the view of the sea and mountains from every angle of the room—even the bed—I could hardly keep back the tears. It was as if the Lord smiled and said, "This is what you asked for when you spoke to Viola." It was God's very precious gift.

It is difficult to express adequately how much my family at home meant to me during those six months. How I reached out for strength that had been completely expended in that long, dark valley of those months. My sisters and their families were wonderful and I could not thank the Lord enough for what their love and care meant when I needed it so much.

I tried to find relaxation and strength in creative and physical work out in the open in my sister's garden in

Vancouver. Her husband, George Sourisseau, was a great gardener. I loved to see God's earth and to see resurrection and new life in the 113 strawberry plants that we planted, in the joy of landscaping, digging, and caring for the rock gardens and flower beds. The work was wonderful, but I became discouraged because only a couple of hours would be all I could take. I worked intensely with almost everything in me, and if I worked a bit too long or hard, I could not sleep all night. I thought I was not "mounting up" as quickly as I should and felt frustrated because the relaxed strength wasn't coming as I expected. I did not realize that what had been expended could not be recovered quickly in a few weeks.

After a month it began to come, and with it a new realization of the Savior's love and care, and the Holy Spirit's ministry of strength to my soul. I will never forget the morning when after tossing most of the night a phrase popped up, "Lil, stop struggling." I was trying to understand and reach out for strength. His message to me was "Do not wrestle, just nestle."

The meaning of the verses in Hebrews, chapter nine came into focus as I read the foundational truth of Christ not only being in us, but the wonderful truth in verses 9–12 in being for us. The truth that Christ was not only *in* us, but *for* us reached down in my depths. I realized that I needed this desperately. I suppose only those who have gone through such an experience can realize what it meant to be reminded then of Deuteronomy 31:8, where God spoke with such positive assurance that He, the God of heaven, would never leave or forsake us.

Exhaustion and weariness slowly gave way and strength began to trickle in through the love, care and prayers of

Audrey Beckett Visiting the Deaf Hostel in Aurangabad

My Honeysuckle Girl, Shalini, Helper in Hostel, Singing with the Deaf Girls in the Hostel in Evening Prayers, in Dresses made by Deaf Girls in Tailoring Class

Deaf Camp, November '96, Pune

Years of Service Reflect God's Glory as Clearly as the Perfect image of the Taj. G. Fletcher with O. Dowsett, Secretary of New Zealand Mukti Council, and L. Doerksen Are Standing Beside It

Madhubala and Her Husband and Family Came for Christmas in 1995 with Ten Boxes of Gifts for Her Honeysuckle Sisters and for the Deaf. Here Madhbala leads the Singing on Christmas Morning at our three-day Honeysuckle Reunion

Lil with Aunt Annie and Her Sister Rosella. **BACK ROW:** Walter, Rosella's Husband, Harold and Viola, George and Mabel, Erna and Brother John

Arvind and Tara and Baby Jacob, 1988

Our First Deaf Camp—Lil Teaching a Song. Arvind Playing the Organ

Pune Deaf Sunday School in Pune

Deaf Camp in Nasrapur, Dr. Cathie Rice, Speaker—1990

Rocky Hillside, with Security Guard's Shack, Fenced In Before Construction

Planting 200 Trees on Deaf Centre Property Donated by Government

Lifting Out the Rock That was Blasted in Well

Miracle Well Lifting Out Rock with Engineer Len Hereema

Pump House, Store Room, and Security Guard's Apartment Going Up

Mahadik, Security Guard and Wife Surekha, with Little Suhas ("Great Joy") after 15 Years of Marriage— the Miracle Baby

Our Staff Quarters Nearing Completion. Six-foot Wall with Six Barbed Wires on Top

Construction of Administrative Building at Deaf Center—Pune

Bombay Deaf Fellowship at YMCA Every Saturday for Deaf Young People and Deaf Couples

Dolly Leading Prayers in Tailoring Class

Deaf Tailoring Class, 1997. Jyoti in Purple Dress

Tailoring Girls in Class

Lillian and Tara with Deaf Tailoring Class at Staff Quarters

Ajit, Avinash, and Another Fellow Who Stayed After Camp for Two-Week Deeper Bible Study, Learning how to Sew Shirts During their Two-Hour Free Time

Deaf Young Peoples Camp in Nasik with Sunny—November 1996. Veerbala, one of Lillian's Honeysuckle Girls, Leads Song

Staff at Nasik Deaf Camp. Bruce Schwalbe, Deaf Missionary was the Speaker

Bombay Camp—Singing with Signs

Bombay Deaf Fellowship Retreat— Listening to God's Word

After Camp, Some of the Deaf Young People Come to Our Home for Several Weeks of More Bible Study

Young Fellow at Nagpur Deaf Camp Teaching a Song

Deaf Couples' and Families' Camp—Pune

Deaf Young People Come to Our Home for Jacob's Birthday. How They Love Singing

Arvin, Tara, Lillian, Nanda, with Jimmy, and Jacob

Hostel for Deaf Girls in Aurangabad. Yellow Van, God's Loving Gift Given by Marcus Robertson, MFD Canadian Board Member

Maya and Sindhu Pradhan when They Came to the Deaf Hostel

Sindhu and Maya Now

School for Deaf Girls in Aurangabad

Deaf Girls in Aurangabad School Class

Deaf Girls Listening to Bible Lesson in Hostel in Aurangabad

Deaf School for Girls in Aurangabad—exercises

Beema (CENTRE) *So Happy Now, in Spoon and Lemon Race*

dear ones who surrounded me. Complete rest and relaxation in the beauty and comfort of that seaside home overlooking Vancouver's beautiful harbor, snow-capped mountains and Gulf islands was God's balm and therapy for both physical and spiritual renewal. The soothing rhythmic constancy of the waves that the tides washed in and out of the shore just below my window day and night, assured me of the faithful constant order and love of God that never changes. The magnificent panoramic view of sea, mountains, sunset and sunrise framed by the large windows in my room where I spent so many hours with the Lord in resting, reading, meditation and prayer, brought a renewed revelation of our Lord's greatness and omnipotent strength.

It was there that the Lord through Isaiah 40:29–31, revealed the secret of strength. Through a message by Dr. Stephen Olford printed in *Christianity Today* on these verses, the Holy Spirit helped me to recognize the peril of expended strength in service that can result in weariness that leads to weakness and can culminate in utter collapse. Even youth, according to verse 29, can become exhausted and young men can utterly fail and faint. I was not exactly a youth after twenty-one years in India of rewarding, but exhausting, service for the Lord in Mukti! I had not heeded warnings of expended strength without necessary rest.

Together with threatened physical collapse had come an intense burden, conviction and inward yearning for a deeper revelation, and a practical experience of the love of Christ, and a more effective ministry in the power of the Holy Spirit.

"But they that wait upon the Lord shall renew [exchange] their strength . . ." God allowed His Spirit to search me deeply in real agony of soul until His truth could be revealed to me: He was waiting to exchange my weakness for His strength, and all the Lord Jesus Himself is, through our oneness with Him. I had been striving through a sense of failure and weakness to strengthen faith and be renewed by His Spirit. Suddenly I realized that I could do nothing but surrender this weakness to Him. I saw it. I read in 2 Timothy 2:13: "Even when we are too weak to have any faith left, he remains faithful to us and will help us for he cannot disown us who are a part of himself, and he will always carry out His promises to us" (LB). How very precious!

Olive Dowsett, a dear friend of mine, who realized what I had been going through, wrote something I will never forget in a letter to me. She said, "Don't wrestle, just nestle in His Everlasting love." At last I understood—that was it! He became my strength. According to Deuteronomy 31:6, I could safely nestle in His loving assurance: "Be strong! Be courageous! . . . He will neither fail you nor forsake you" (LB). The repetition of this again in verse eight made His promise doubly sure.

I had waited on Him patiently in the long months of weakness and darkness— and they had seemed so long. But He had inclined Himself and revealed that "beauty and strength are in His sanctuary" (Psalm 96:6).

With my weakness exchanged for divine strength, there came enduement with power by the Holy Spirit to fulfill His will in Mukti and wherever He chose to lead me.

What joy to find myself in flight again towards India on wings of obedient submission. How different was my return from Canada on September 10, with gratitude in my heart for all the loving care and kindness that had been shown to me, and a deep new joy and rest in Him who is my strength, Gladys Fletcher and another friend were at Bombay Airport to meet me. Though the Bombay heat was intense, and it took over two hours to get through immigration and customs formalities, there was such a deep sense of relaxation, peace and God's loving kindness.

When I arrived at the Kedgoan station, our two-year-old Honeysuckle, Vidyulata, greeted me with a kiss and a cheer of *Jai* (victory). I could hardly hold back the tears of joy that I had been able to exchange my weakness for His strength as garlands were put around my neck. At the Mukti gate young and old sang songs of greeting.

My room was so clean and fragrant with flowers. I was *home* and I could not wait to kneel down beside my bed to thank God for His miracle. I knew that I no longer needed to wrestle—just nestle.

Chapter Ten

The Prayer Tower

Each day at Mukti was full of surprises from the Father's hand. For among this community of children, older women and missionaries, new groups began springing up. Some were praying, while others were sewing and were giving for missions from the little they had. In fact, kindness dripped like dew from the living hand of God through His children at this wonderful place.

Ruth Akka, the matron of our family then, shared with me happy news one morning about Bobbie, one of our five-year-old girls. Having heard the school children talk of the border troubles between India and China in the north, Bobbie had asked, "Are the Chinese soldiers in New Delhi yet?" Surprised, Ruth assured her that they were not.

Bobbie was also concerned about our baby twins—Veedula and Mroodula—who had come to us recently. "If the Communists come," she said, "they will cry and cling to you, won't they?" Then Bobbie added, "But I won't cry, Akka, because I'm saved. I'll tell them so and even if they kill me, it's all right. I'll go straight to Jesus because I belong to Him."

Ruth's voice quivered with deep-felt emotion as she added, "Moushi, I could not keep back the tears to hear that a five-year-old was ready to die for Jesus."

Could any green light hold such a great challenge to press forward with the message of the power of the gospel in Mukti? I went straight to the Prayer Tower for a time alone with God, to thank the Heavenly Father for such faith among our children. I was glad for that tower where praise as well as deep requests for prayer could be made by all of those in the mission.

As I climbed up the steps into the prayer room that was above the passageway in the middle of the stone residences that Ramabai built for the staff, I remembered what a blessing it had been to be involved in the

Prayer Tower with International Conference Delegates and Mukti Staff

creation of this tower.

Ramabai had planned for it to be a prayer tower when she had designed the mission center. She wanted it to be a place where the girls and the staff could go up to have private times of prayer. It was never completed in her lifetime, or for many years afterwards.

I used to look at the unfinished tower and wish so much that it could have that special prayer room and thus fulfill her initial vision. But as the years passed by, we seemed no closer to completing the project.

Memorial donations sent to me at the mission when my father died challenged me to help make that prayer sanctuary a reality. Then my brother Sam passed away from complications with stomach ulcers, and more memorial donations were made towards the project.

When Anne Monson, one of my best friends and a wonderful prayer warrior, went to her reward, again there were donations that I could put towards the Prayer Tower project. This was enough for the work to begin. It was fitting that the gifts that came in memory of Anne were put towards it, as she had been the general secretary for some time of the Canadian council of the Ramabai Mukti Mission, which I had helped to establish on my first furlough. Anne had visited me in India and was glad to meet Suhasani of our Honeysuckle Family, whom she and her physically-challenged daughter had been generously supporting.

A Hindu friend of mine, Mr. A. Dhekney, who was a builder, offered to draw up the plans for the tower. It was a real joy when I saw the work completed and was able to climb up one of the two sets of steps on the two sides of the tower that went up to the lovely little prayer room. Soon people from Mukti could go up there on their own or as part of a group to get away for times of prayer.

In honor of my father, Sam, Anne, and my sister Sylvia who had also since passed away, a brass plate was erected on the wall dedicating the room to their memory.

Interesting Encounters

We all knew only too well at the mission that prayer had to be the key if we were to succeed in our work in India. It was especially vital when we would go on long deputation journeys in our new Volkswagen, because of the dangers all along the way.

One exciting trip to the eastern coast of India was with Leelabai, one of our graduates from Bible seminary. Leela was my efficient and dedicated helper on these trips. In Andhra Pradesh, we visited many interesting institutions, churches and schools, where we had a great response and wonderful fellowship, sharing about Pandita Ramabai's great faith and the work of the "Home of Salvation"—Mukti Mission.

Although travel was difficult at the best of times in India, it was virtually impossible to make any kind of time or progress, especially on the Grand Trunk Highway, a vast highway between Madras and Calcutta. The problem was there were scores of lumbering black water buffaloes that monopolized the road. We would travel a few furlongs only to encounter hundreds of these and other animals. They were stretched right across and it seemed that the highway had been provided just for them.

The Ambling "Brake Inspectors"

We called the buffaloes "brake inspectors" because they certainly did test them. We would just get speed up to thirty-five or forty miles an hour when we were upon another herd going out to graze or ambling home along the highway.

The buffaloes always made us slow right down or even come to a full stop. They never turned to the side of the road until they had a good look at us. They seemed to let us know that the road was theirs, as if questioning and wondering how good our brakes were.

But this tortuous travel schedule was rewarded with wonderful fellowship, especially in one church—the Baptist church of Ongole. Pastor Samuel's mother had visited us at the Mukti mission and was very interested in what we shared about our big church that seated over 2,000 that Ramabai had built on the site. Pastor Samuel's grandparents were the fruit of a great mass movement in the work of missions in that part of India. He shared with us that where there had been great barrenness, God's Spirit began to move in the late 1800s, and thousands upon thousands had become Christians.

As a result the church was founded and grew in an astounding way. We discovered that the Ongole church was, at the time we visited it, possibly the largest Baptist church in the world, with over 20,000 members. This may sound impossible for India, but we saw it with our own eyes. On one Sunday alone, 2,222 had been baptized in that church.

A missionary named Mr. Clough started a relief project with his evangelistic work and a great canal was dug that brought great prosperity to the state. The people then were mostly from a backward background. It was thrilling to see their grandchildren now with all kinds of degrees behind their names, leaders in the church and in places of authority everywhere.

The Miracle Breakdown

Another tour that was of great interest was one of our state when we traveled to northern Maharashtra. Although the Volkswagen had been carefully gone over before we had begun, we had a breakdown while going through Poona, due to a faulty condenser. The Lord let it happen right in front of the Das Garage where it was fixed with no great difficulty. We were so thankful that it did not happen in the middle of the river we crossed later or in some lonely place where there would have been no one to help. We lost two hours waiting for the condenser to be replaced, but it saved us hours of concern had it happened elsewhere.

At a meeting at Pimpalner, we praised God for the sweetest fellowship with the husbands of some of the Mukti girls, one of whom loved talking about the Lord and expressed such gratitude for the wife that God had given him.

He said, "My, your girls from Mukti sure know how to love! She is such a good wife." He went on to explain that God had given them a lovely family. It was good to hear that our Mukti girls had benefited from and reflected the love they had received.

That night our meeting in the local church was a precious time of fellowship, and the "stand-in" ministry of the Holy Spirit was great.

The next day over sixty-five village women attended our conference. I was concerned that my message might be too deep; the women were such simple "newly entered in" ones of the Bhil- or Mouchie-speaking mountain tribespeople. I need not have worried. It was wonderful to see their hunger and an eagerness for the Word in their faces. There was such a consciousness of God's presence and of the Holy Spirit teaching these women.

Les and Verna Buhler, missionaries from the Central Heights Church in Abbottsford, were in charge of this work and doing a wonderful outreach there. They took up an offering for Mukti and these dear people gave the equivalent of twenty dollars, which was a lot for them. They also provided a sack of rice for our Mukti children.

A MEASURED PILGRIMAGE

These were days of blessing as we visited churches and many other places of that area of Dhulia, Malegaon, and Jalgaon. It was on the highway on our way home that we had an unusual encounter. For there we met a woman measuring her length on the road.

"Oh Leela! What's that on the road?" I exclaimed as I slammed on the brakes of the van. Swerving to miss the object in front of the car, I almost hit a bullock cart trundling towards us on the highway.

"Whew! That was close! I barely missed her," I gasped as I pulled the Volkswagen van over to the side of the road and stopped. I wiped the perspiration from my forehead. A person could run into anything on those Indian roads. Usually it was goats or cows, water buffaloes or sheep, even sleeping dogs or beggars. But this was different!

"I've seen women doing that in the villages or around a temple," I said "But this is the first time I've seen a woman on the highway like that." My voice was shaky and I gave a deep sigh of relief that I had not run over the woman.

Leela, my Indian companion, leaned forward and shuddered.

"She is measuring her length along the road on her way to some holy temple, I am sure," she said. "Who knows how far she has come? Come on let's get out and see if we can talk to her."

I switched off the ignition and climbed down with Leela. We motioned to the woman to stop. She had a little stick in

Sharing God's Love with the Lombardi Tribal People

her land. Lying face down on the road and reaching as far as she could, the woman scratched a little mark in the dust. Then she stood up, put her toes where the mark was and lay down flat on the road again while repeating over and over the name of her Hindu god. Making another mark as far as her arm would stretch, down she would go again. Up and down, up and down, she struggled like this along the road. Leela tried to motion for the woman to stop.

"*Bai* [*woman*]," she said tenderly as she touched the woman's arm, "Bai, listen to me. Where are you going and why are you doing all of this?"

The woman had neither noticed the van, nor seen us

Woman Measuring Her Length on Road to Holy Temple in Sholapur

coming to her side. She stopped and looked at us with surprise, still muttering the name of her god.

"Stop and tell us what you're doing, Bai," said Leela gently as she helped her come to the side of the road and sit down. "You look so tired. Have you come a long way?"

"Yes, I have come from Sholapur," she answered wearily.

"And where are you going? You have already come such a long way."

Leela looked at the woman closely. She felt sorry for her. When the woman said, "I'm going to Pandhrapur," Leela gasped.

"To Pandhrapur!" she explained. "But that's a long, long way and you look exhausted already. Have you eaten? Why are you making this pilgrimage?"

"My fate is bad. We are poor," she said. "I have worked in the fields to help provide food for our family. But my eyes are going bad. The man whose land we farm sends us to the fields, but I cannot see the weeds. I try my best, but I cannot pull the weeds if I cannot see them. How can I help it? My eyes get worse and worse and I see less and less. What will happen if I go completely blind? I faithfully worship at the temple. The priest says the only hope for my sight is to make this pilgrimage to Pandhrapur, and then our god Vithoba will take the curse off my eyes so I can see. I have made a vow that I will gain Vithoba's favor by going and making an offering at his temple in Pandhrapur. Is there any other hope?" The poor woman raised her hands helplessly.

Leela put her arm on the woman's shoulder. "Yes, there is hope," she said. "Have you ever heard of the living God whose name is Jesus?" she asked.

"No, no, never. Who is he?" asked the woman eagerly. "We have many gods, but I have not heard of that one. Can he help me?"

"He is not like your gods of wood and stone. He is the living God who loves you. His name is Jesus Christ and . . ."

"Oh, yes, yes," the woman interrupted as her face lit up. "Krishna, I know. He will help?" she said.

"No, no, not Krishna. It's Christ, the Lord Jesus Christ. Can you say His name? It is a beautiful, sweet name. He is the God of love and He loves you. He has power to heal you."

The woman drew in her breath as she listened to the story of Christ's suffering on the cross for her sins because of His great, great love for her.

"But how could he love me? How could he know me? I have never seen him or done anything for him." The woman lifted her troubled eyes to Leela.

"But He has seen you. He knows you through and through. He created you and has known you all along. In spite of your sins He loves you and died for you."

Leela took out some Bible booklets and tracts and asked the woman if there was anyone in her home who could read. The woman was just telling her about her children when two teenagers came along the road. One was carrying a baby.

"Oh, look!" she said. "There they are! My son and daughter are coming with me and have brought my baby. They had stopped at the last village to rest and drink tea."

"Have you had tea or food?" Leela asked with concern.

"Oh no, I cannot eat or the gods will not accept my vow. Three times a day my children must give me fruit which they buy in the villages. I can chew this and spit it out, but I must not swallow anything."

When Leela and I saw the woman take the baby and open her blouse to feed it, we looked at one another, for we were worried. How could she feed the baby when she could not eat for many days?

"Have you had tea? Can we get you something to drink?" we asked her.

"My children have brought water. Sometimes my stomach begs for a cup of tea. I can only rinse my mouth with it, but not swallow. Otherwise it is not acceptable to the god."

Leela's heart ached. How was the woman going to complete her long pilgrimage, which would take at least several more weeks, without taking in any food or drink? How could she have milk for her baby if she could not get enough liquids into her body? Already the baby looked weak and listless.

"My son can read," she said proudly. "Give him the books about this God of love. He will read to us."

Eagerly, the sad-faced teenager took the book and looked at it. Leela shared the good news with him. She told him that God's book would help him to know the living Savior.

Then Leela sat down in front of the woman.

"Bai," she said earnestly, "don't go any further on the pilgrimage. You will never reach Pandhrapur. There is hope for you without it. Your only hope for this life and for the next world is the Lord Jesus Christ, the God of love who made such a great sacrifice in that pilgrimage to the cross for you. If you will take His name and believe in Him with all your heart, He will give you His life and He can heal your eyes if you pray to Him. Go back to your home. He will be with you always."

"Your words sound sweet to my ears," said the woman, with a look of longing that touched Leela's heart.

"Believe them," Leela reassured her, "they are true. Give me your stick. Take the name of the Lord Jesus Christ. Trust

Him. He will give you new life. And He can heal you. Go back."

The woman talked to her children, looked up longingly at Leela and said finally, "We will go back. God has sent you. He can heal my eyes. I will say the name. My tongue does not turn around it easily. Tell me again. I must not forget it."

Again and again she repeated the name of Jesus. Then with determination she looked up at Leela and me, gave us her little stick with which she had been marking her length on the road, and started off with her children, back to their home in Sholapur. She walked along softly saying the name of Jesus over and over again so she would not forget.

Leela could not get that poor woman out of her mind. She thought of her and of so many others like her in India. How they needed the hope that is found only in the Lord Jesus Christ! How could they hear His name unless someone told them? She had dedicated her life to the Lord Jesus Christ many years before. She knew He wanted her to bring the message of His love to her people.

THE SOAPY BRAKE FLUID

The Honeysuckle Family had so many wonderful outings. One was to the Mahableshwar Hills. After a wonderful time, we were on our way home down the mountain, the girls singing with glee at the top of their voices.

We had hardly passed the first big curve when I called out to them, "Girls, stop singing and pray! The brakes on our Volkswagen have suddenly given way." There were many trucks and buses winding their way up through the narrow road that we would have to pass. I quickly switched into first gear and oh, how I prayed, along with the girls, that God would take us safely down the hill. When we came to a spot where there had been a rock slide, it seemed impossible. If a car had come from the other side, we would have gone right over the side and over the steep drop as there were no guard rails. Somehow, miraculously, God took us down the mountain, though we had many other close calls.

When we reached the bottom of the mountain, I drove slowly, anxious to get to a service station to have the brakes tested and fixed. It was a holiday and not only the first one, but every service station along the seventy-mile road back to Poona was closed. I knew I could not go through the city of Poona in that condition to get home to Mukti. As we prayed, I suddenly spotted off the road, almost hidden from view, a service station that looked open. The attendant told me there was nothing he could do except to pour a soap solution into the empty brake fluid section. He assured me that this soap mixture would help me get through busy Poona. We prayed, and to our joy, we found it was working! We miraculously got all through the busy traffic of Poona and the forty-five miles beyond to our home in Kedgeon.

Our staff in Mukti could not believe that we had managed to come home safely when they heard the story. The girls still remember it as a miracle of our Father in Heaven who so wonderfully answered our prayers.

Chapter Eleven

A Message for
The Dalai Lama

Benares (or Varanasi) is a sacred city for Hindus. Located in Uttar Pradesh State, northern India, on the north bank of the Ganges River, the city contains more than 1,500 temples and mosques. Hindu pilgrims come from all over India and the world to bathe in the "holy" Ganges waters that they believe will help give them forgiveness of sins.

So, it was a surprise to see in front of the Buddhist *stupa* (*temple*) in this predominately Hindu city, hundreds of Tibetan refugees dressed in their multi-colored robes.

Many were turning prayer wheels and chanting in a language that I didn't understand, while others stood expectantly and reverently near a car clutching marigolds to throw into the path of the vehicle.

I was in Benares with Olive Dowsett, general secretary of the mission in New Zealand and Gladys Fletcher, the Mukti superintendent, as part of a research trip that we were making.

"What is the special occasion for all these people?" I asked one of the lamas (Buddhist monks of Tibet or Mongolia).

"You don't know that the Dalai Lama is visiting the temple?" he asked. "He will be coming out any minute and these people are here to have a *darshan* (a religious sight) of him," he added.

I had followed with sadness the plight of the Tibetan people and their religious leader, who up until 1959 had also been their temporal ruler. Each Dalai Lama is believed to be the reincarnation of his predecessor. When one dies the new incarnation is sought among newborn boys. The child is identified by his ability to pick out possessions of the former Dalai Lama from a group of objects.

This, the fourteenth Dalai Lama, was born Tenzin Gyatso in 1935 and was installed in 1940. He remained in Tibet from the Chinese takeover in 1950 until 1959, when he fled to India following an abortive Tibetan revolt against Chinese Communist rule. He established a Tibetan government in exile in Dharmshala and has worked to preserve Tibetan arts, scriptures and medicine.

One of the lamas went into the temple to inform him that a group of three Western ladies were outside. He returned a few minutes later and we were surprised when he said in Hindi, "His Holiness would like to see you. You can have a three-minute interview with his Holiness."

In a state of shock, we followed the lama into the temple, and there we saw the Dalai Lama sitting cross-legged on a mat on the floor.

"Ladies, please sit," he indicated as he pointed to a mat in front of him. As we did, a friendly smile lit up his face. We had expected some small talk, but his face became serious as he asked, "What message do you have for me?"

We had not expected such a comment. "Sir, Miss Fletcher and I here are Christian missionaries working in India and this other lady is Miss Olive Dowsett from New Zealand, who represents our mission there, " I began.

He smiled and bowed his head towards each one of us. "Your holiness," I continued, "the message we have for you is that our God loves you and so do we. We serve this great God and His only begotten Son, Jesus Christ."

He thanked me for that "message," and then Olive interjected. "Your holiness, I have a prayer meeting in my home in New Zealand and I want to tell you that we pray regularly for you and the Tibetan people."

As she spoke the Dalai Lama listened intently and smiled gently. We were so thrilled that in those few minutes we had been able to share the gospel with him. It was an amazing interview.

I realized that our three minutes were now up, so I said, "Your Holiness, would you mind if we had a word of prayer to our God for you."

"Oh, please do," he said.

So I closed my eyes and began asking the Lord to bless this man and his people.

With that we knew it was time for us to leave and we stood to our feet. We were not prepared for what happened next as the Dalai Lama followed us outside. As soon as he appeared, like a streak of lightning, all of those hundreds of Tibetan pilgrims fell flat to the ground, showing their deep devotion to the one they believed to be god. Then, as the car began to move away, they rose to their feet and began throwing marigolds in front of it. The Dalai Lama bowed and smiled through the window. The three of us had to pinch ourselves about what had just occurred.

WIDOWS OF THE TEMPLES

After catching our breath we began visiting some of the Hindu temples in Benares. We had already been in several when I asked Gladys, "Did you notice how many older women seem to be living in these temples?"

She nodded and explained that widows are blamed for their husband's death and so have to spend the rest of their lives in a temple to atone for "having caused their husband's death."

Gladys added, "Each day they go from the temple to the Ganges and bathe in it to try to wash away the cause of their sad fate."

I discovered that this was seen to be a step forward from a previous practice of the widow being expected to allow herself to be burned alive by falling on her late husband's funeral pyre!

We stood at the side of the three-mile river-bank in the city and watched thousands of pilgrims already in the water and others picking their way down brick bathing steps into the sacred Ganges.

Just being in Benares made me realize the role that India has played in the history of religion. It is the birthplace of Hinduism, Buddhism, Jainism and Sikhism, though it is today a secular state and its constitution guarantees religious tolerance of all groups.

Not only is religion diverse in India, but its people are also. This land that I love so much has one of the world's most varied populations with most of the major races represented. Over thousands of years countless groups migrated onto the subcontinent. Many of these groups have maintained distinctive cultures through the ages. India's tribal peoples and the large number of later migrant groups represent a wide variety of physical types and cultural traditions.

One group that I came across during a trip were the *Lombardis* (a gypsy-type tribe). There are over a million of these in Andhra Pradesh alone and over 800 were settled in one village. By the power of the Holy Spirit, God filled our days with the special blessing and the deep joy of seeing a number of these people gloriously saved. And how we prayed that God would keep them and shield them.

These days were strategic and full of challenge. I wanted to be my best for the Lord in the time He gave us, to be in line with His purposes and to be used as He saw fit. How I prayed for God to direct and guide for the right place for an opportunity for rest. The hammer and sickle signs and monuments were constant reminders in that state that that day was our opportunity for the Lord.

The Hindu Pilgrims

The major religion of the Indian subcontinent is Hinduism. The word derived from an ancient Sanskrit term meaning "dwellers by the Indus River," a reference to the location of India's earliest known civilization in what is now Pakistan. Apart from animism, from which it may have partly derived, Hinduism is one of the oldest of the world's religions. It dates back more than 3,000 years, though its present forms are of more recent origin. Today more than ninety percent of the world's Hindus live in India.

Hinduism is so unlike any other religion that it is difficult to define it with any precision. It has no founder and its origins are lost in a very distant past. It does not have one holy book, but several. There is no single body of doctrine. Instead there is a great diversity of belief and practice. It is a religion that worships over 300 million gods. Yet it also adheres to the view that there is only one god, called Brahma. All other divinities are aspects of the one absolute and unknowable Brahma.

Another distinctive feature of Hinduism is belief in the transmigration of souls—of reincarnation. Association with this belief is the conviction that all living things are part of the same essence. Individuals pass through cycles of birth and death. This means, they believe, that an individual soul may return many times in human, animal or even vegetable form. What a person does in the present life will affect the next life.

I saw hundreds of Hindu pilgrims who were on their way to Pandhrapur, about 100 miles from our place. Several of us Mukti missionaries and Bible women drove there on one occasion to witness this Hindu religious festival and share the message of our living Savior. It was an incredible sight for us. Every road and riverbed was covered like flies with pilgrims on their way to the festival. The trains were also packed to capacity with these people. When our little

Pilgrims Bathing in Ganges River in Benares

group arrived in Pandhrapur at midnight, we discovered that every bit of available ground or roadway was covered with sleeping pilgrims, many who had come many hundreds of miles. Some we were told had walked long distances to be there.

One amazing sight that we saw in that city was a man who had rolled himself all the way from his village many miles away. The pieces of rubber tire tied around his elbows and knees had worn through and blood marked the roadway each time he rolled over. Not only the tire, but also his elbow and knee pads, had worn through. Barely making his way past the countless idols and shrines towards the great temple of the black god, he was feverishly muttering out loud the names of his gods in his eager effort to gain merit for heaven. He stopped to listen as we shared with him the love of God for him and the way of joy and forgiveness through the Lord Jesus.

We were up very early next morning—before five o'clock—and we were able to witness at that auspicious moment the shallow, dirty Bhima River swarming with 60,000 pilgrims who were bathing, washing their clothes, and drinking all of the water they could, seeking to wash away their sins and to gain merit for salvation. My heart yearned with the compassion of our Lord Jesus Christ that they would one day find the real Savior.

THE CHALLENGE OF POVERTY

Coming from a land of plenty, India also presented me with the challenge of extreme poverty of so many of these dear people. Yet, in their destitution, we saw them sacrifice their offerings at thousands of shrines, idols and temples that swallowed up their small, scanty earnings and often their very living. This made me wonder if Christians were willing to make such sacrifices for their Lord!

There was also the challenge of the women of India. In the West, we know only too well the love, comfort and ease of a fine Christian home. But in India there are the millions of village women, India's burden bearers. They live in small, one-roomed mud huts and must raise their families and often toil in the fields from dawn until dusk. Beginning each day with the worship of the household gods with their husbands, they seek to appease the gods, provoke their favor and yearn on for the hope of salvation and peace and love.

Yes, not only did we have a message for the Dalai Lama, but for them also.

Chapter Twelve

AN IMPERFECT
SACRIFICE

What, I wondered, *could be keeping my Honeysuckles?* They had not raced home and into my room after the Sunday afternoon service with their usual excited, "Where do we go on our walk today, Moushi?" When there was no response to my call to "Come quickly," but instead more noise than usual, I began to worry. I stepped over to the family room to see what was wrong. Surely there was not a quarrel or some other problem, I hoped.

"Please no," I quietly prayed, "don't let anything spoil our happy weekly walk."

As I stepped into the room the little ones rushed toward me, grabbed my hands and giggled. What was going on? Then I saw it! For there on our "floor table," everything was laid out for a party. There were beautiful flowers, a picture they had painted, promises from God's Word and an inscribed prayer. My Honeysuckle Family had arranged a beautiful program to remind me of my twenty-fifth anniversary in India!

We sat cross-legged on the floor in front of our plates laden with dainties they had prepared when I thought they were resting. As I looked at them through a prism of tears, I realized that a quarter of a century of my life had passed, in which the Lord had privileged me to live and work with these children in India.

When God had called me through His Word in Isaiah 42:6, He said, "I the LORD have called you in righteousness and will hold your hand, and will keep you, and give you for a covenant of the people and a light of the nations." At that moment, I did not understand all it would involve, but I did know that I could trust Him. How faithfully He had kept me!

Looking around the room and thinking of my "spiritual children" and the others that God had given me, my heart was moved with deep gratitude and joy for the privilege of being a light for Him in India. In our Honeysuckle Family at that time, He had entrusted me with twenty-six precious girls—five of whom were married. We already then had four grandchildren. God promised in Isaiah to keep them, too. "This is my promise," He had said, "My Holy Spirit shall not leave them, and they shall want good and hate the wrong—they and their children's children forever" (Isaiah 59:19, LB).

How much this promise meant to me as I prepared for my next furlough. The Lord proved His power to keep when I was prepared to leave.

CHRISTMAS IN BOMBAY

So we could all be together as a family at Christmas in 1976, we had arranged to spend a few days in Bombay until my departure for furlough. Our girls in college, nurses' training, and those who were married, had all agreed to travel to be with us for a real family get-together.

But the time turned out very differently from what we had planned!

Ruth Akka (Big Sister), the matron-mother of our Honeysuckle Family, had helped me bring up all the girls, many of whom had come as deserted children, often more dead than alive. She also had helped me teach them with a true mother's heart.

Ruth had first come to Mukti as a deserted baby. After she attended the Mukti School she worked as a nurse-mother in the Buds compound. She came to be the matron-mother of my family when we took what were left of the Buds in the nursery after the family system came into being.

When Ruth was twenty-eight, she felt that it was time for her to think of marriage. I managed to arrange a fine marriage with a young man who was active in teaching the Word—the Bible—in his local church. When they had two children and both of them were deaf, she was devastated. She tried to remember if she had perhaps been too strict sometimes or unfair, and now God was punishing her with first a boy and then a girl who were both completely deaf.

I tried to comfort her by saying that God was not like that, that He was a God of love. "Perhaps He could not have trusted anybody else with two deaf children," I told her. This was an encouragement for her, and we together tried to find medical help and schools for the deaf.

Bombay was then a city of more than six million people. There was no classified telephone directory or any way to find where the deaf schools were located. For a while, she went to hospitals for help and direction for the children. Each diagnosis was different. It wasn't until the boy was five and the girl three, that we were able to locate deaf schools. In our state they did not teach sign language in deaf schools, but only lip reading. Deaf children had to be admitted before the age of three, so they could have a foundation for lip reading. Consequently, they refused to accept the boy who was five, but the little girl was placed in the school.

The school was far from home. Ruth had to travel more than two hours in the morning and two hours in the evening to bring her home. She was finally able to find a place where deaf boys were being taught near her home, but the teachers were very inefficient and half the time the children just lolled around on the verandah.

It was nearly Christmas of 1976 and time for my furlough. I had decided to leave on New Year's Eve so I could spend Christmas with all my Honeysuckle Family in Bombay and then they could see me off. We rented a room for five days in a high school hostel there. This was so that all my married girls and those in college, in nurses' training and in special boarding schools, could come and have a little time together with me before I left.

There were thirty-four of us, and we had planned it all right down to the food and the outings that we would have. I also saved the money gifts that I had received for Christmas and was able to get a special price with the airlines so that they could have the half-hour airplane ride to Poona after I had left.

Time had been set aside for Christmas shopping on Christmas Eve. This was not to happen. Instead that morning, we found that Ruth's boy Melind was missing from the deaf school. Ruth was four month's pregnant at the time and she was devastated because they couldn't find him anywhere. They felt he had been stolen.

The school was located in the Thane area of Bombay. We spent the whole day praying and trying to help find him in a city of over six million. We purchased no gifts, because we could not spend a happy Christmas wondering if the child was dead or not.

Children are sometimes stolen off the streets in India to be used as slave labor. They have also been used as human sacrifices. That week the newspapers had run a story of some Hindu religious orthodox contractors who had used these children as living sacrifices to be put in the foundations of bridges and big buildings when they were not sure of the integrity of the structures. They hoped that through the sacrifices, the gods would protect the structures.

At 10:30 P.M. on Christmas Eve, a miracle happened. The police phoned to say that they thought they had found Melind. What had possibly happened was that when the kidnappers discovered that the boy was deaf and also slightly handicapped from a birth injury, they decided not to kill him as they were afraid that the gods would not accept an imperfect sacrifice.

Whatever the reason, the deaf-mute boy had been dumped twenty miles from his home, eleven railway stations in between.

He was left at midnight in the railway station. The police found him crying and desperate and took him to a remand home to try to locate his family. As he had been reported, his parents were soon contacted. Ruth's husband, Sadanand, and I went to the remand home, but the police

Melind—So Happy After the "Imperfect Sacrifice"

refused to let us see the boy that night. The rule was that the child had to be identified by the parents in court.

Being Christmas, this identification was set for December 27. Even though the officials did not want to show him to us on Christmas Day, we said we would not leave the remand home until we saw him. It was my little "brag" book, where I keep all the pictures of my girls, that was to solve the situation. First I asked the Hindu man in charge if he had a family. "Yes, I do," he answered.

"Well," I said, "at your big festival, Diwali (Festival of Lights), when your family comes for a feast, if one of your children were missing and had not been located, would you eat the food that had been prepared for your feast?"

The man answered, "No, of course not."

Then I showed him my book—the children that I had brought up. I told him how they were all sitting waiting for a word from us with Christmas dinner in front of them, but they could not eat it without knowing if their sister's child was dead or alive. "Here is the picture," I said. "Here is the father. Do you think we can eat until we know if this father's child is alive?" I asked.

Without saying another word, he left the room. The Hindu man looked up the child's number in the file. A few moments later, he brought the boy and his father ran and swept him up into his arms. I then hugged him. He was going to cry and we told him not to cry as we had brought him sweets and fruit. Then later, we went to the courts and got him.

My furloughs were filled with meetings and sharing about the wonderful work of God in that great Home of Salvation.

When I went to India in 1950, the American council of the Ramabia Mukti Mission sent me. Now we were two Canadian missionaries in India, Anne Siemens and I. It was felt we needed to reach out to our Canadian friends and churches and start a council in Canada. During my furlough I was able to establish the Canadian council.

Anne Monson went to the Briercrest Bible Institute with me, was my best high school pal and my roommate, and we both sang in the Briercrest Institute Radio quartet. Anne was always interested in my ministry and supported one of my Honeysuckle girls. She also became a general secretary of the Mukti Canadian council.

Peggy Mackay, another dear friend from my church and a great prayer partner, succeeded Anne as general secretary when Anne passed away. She also made a precious contribution to the ministry.

On a later furlough, when Peggy was very ill and I had gone to see her before I left for India again, I experienced a glimpse of heaven. Her face was aglow as she shared of a wonderful encounter and vision she had recently had. It seemed almost in heavenly language. "Lil," she told me, "while I was praying, I suddenly heard the sound of a rushing stream and the room was filled with light. I saw Jesus standing near my bed and with Him was my dear Murdo (her late husband, whose prayers were always more precious and powerful than any I remember) and also our first-born baby who died in infancy."

Her face aglow, she shared the Savior's message to her. Then she hugged me and we wept together. It was a moment of glory that I shall never forget. After a little precious prayer, she pulled out a beautiful ruby ring from under her pillow. She asked me to wear it—her parting gift to remind me of her love and prayers. It was hard to say goodbye. I was in tears as I left the room and told her daughter Isabel and husband John about the vision she had shared. How wonderful for her to have such assurance as she faced death.

"I think it was meant for us even more," said Isabel. "What a blessed comfort for us! We heard her talking and wondered whom she was talking to. When we went into the room it still seemed aglow, and her face was shining as she shared her vision. It was so real and such a comfort and blessing." Two weeks later, I was informed that she had gone to meet her Savior in heaven. I treasured that last glorious visit with her.

That furlough was especially blessed as I traveled through Canada and the US, meeting many friends who had so faithfully supported the ministry in Mukti and what I was later to become involved with in India. Viola Dand, another dear friend in Seattle, also made a great contribution to the ministry in Mukti when she was the general secretary for some time. Since then she has had a missionary career as an executive secretary, spending short-terms in Peru, at HCJB in Ecuador and in Albania. She was also our secretary for the Maharashtra Fellowship for Deaf council when it was formed.

Later, when I returned from my furlough, I was able to locate Christian deaf schools in other states. Ruth Akka had no training but tried so hard to teach her children about God and His love. But there seemed to be no way she could get across to her two deaf children any spiritual truth to help them to understand God's love and salvation. Mroodula, her daughter, who was attending the Bombay Deaf School, was learning and singing about the Hindu gods and dancing before the idols, like Ganpati and others. She could not understand why she should not bow to them like the other children and could not seem to grasp the thought of the "Jesus God" and His love.

I was able to find a fine Christian deaf school in Bangalore in Karantika State. Mroodula was very happy there and soon understood that Jesus was the living God who loved her. She accepted Him as her Savior and confessed Him in baptism at the Baptist church attached to this boarding school.

Melind was so happy when we finally found a Christian boy's school in another state, Andhra Pradesh. The language was different, the food and everything else seemed different, but he, like his sister, adapted well.

It was a shock then, some months later, when I had a long distance telephone call from the principal of the boy's school from Dornakal, Andhra Pradesh. At first I did not understand when they told me that Melind had gone to glory. When he explained that Melind had a little temperature and on his own he had gone to the well to cool off, for he had seen boys swimming in the large well (which was 30 feet in diameter). He had walked down the steps that had led into the water on the inside of the well with no one around. Because he had never learned to swim, he drowned in the well.

Though it was a sad shock, it was comforting to both his parents and me to know that he had been so happy there and we would meet again in glory.

I was glad that I was able to help Ruth and her husband with these children because it was not easy for them with two deaf children, and another baby boy.

GOD KEPT ME TO MY PROMISE

It was at that time that I promised God that if I had health and strength left when I retired, that I would give the rest of my life for a spiritual ministry to deaf in our state of Maharashtra. There was not any Christian ministry to the deaf of any kind in our whole state.

God kept me to that promise to help the deaf community. Even before I retired, I was preparing for the new deaf ministry. While visiting a major Christian publisher in the US, he suggested that I call the principal of the Tennessee Temple University in Chattanooga, Tennessee, where they had a good Deaf Education Department. He said I should share with him the fact that we did not have a single ministry to the deaf in my state. I did and told him of my burden to help deaf people in my state. He immediately asked me to come and see him, as he was going to meet his board to see about scholarships to their Deaf Education Department. I flew to Chattanooga and our meeting resulted in the presentation of five scholarships so we could send someone to be trained at their Deaf Education College Department.

I had shared with Rita, a teacher in a fine Christian school in New Delhi, who was helping hard of hearing children in her school. The principal of that school was on our Mukti board and when she heard that I had received scholarships from the Tennessee Temple University in Chattanooga, which had an excellent Deaf Education Department, she asked if it would be possible for me to send her so she could have a share in helping us in our ministry to the deaf.

Rita not only had a wonderful time in the college, but she was also able to share about the need for a Christian deaf ministry at different churches in America that later became interested in helping with support.

When Rita returned from the United States, she was shocked to find that her Hindu parents had arranged a wedding and she was to be married within a month. It was to a fine Christian young man, Prem James, who was the assistant director of Far Eastern Broadcasting Company (FEBC) in India. The parents were impressed when Bhakt Singh Chabra, a great man of God, brought this young man and asked them for Rita to be a wife for this fine young man. They were a strict Hindu family, but they knew that Rita would not marry a Hindu man now. They liked Prem and consented to let him marry their daughter. Both Prem and Rita had been led to the Lord and baptized by this great servant of God. Consequently, the wedding was to take place within a month of her return. It was all arranged without her having met him or knowing anything about him.

On arrival back in India, Rita flew down from New Delhi to Poona to see me. We wept and prayed together trying to understand God's ways. He gave us His peace and assurance that all would work out for His glory. When she returned to Delhi she heard that FEBC officials had decided that Prem had to go to Europe for deputation and further training, and would be gone for five months. The wedding was postponed until his return. This meant that Rita could spend those five months with us at the Ramabai Mukti Mission to help me and my girls learn more about deaf psychology and sign language. Another miracle happened. Just at this time our state government had started the first rural deaf school in our state. They opened up the hostel and school right on the edge of our property! We immediately took the girls and started a Sunday school every Sunday afternoon at this deaf school.

As I waited on the Lord in my last month at the mission, I looked to Him for a final confirmation about launching into this deaf ministry.

I had decided to arrange for a deaf camp. I contacted several of the government deaf schools in Poona and

Bombay and invited them each to send fifteen deaf children between the ages of eight and twelve. Rita was coming to help us with this camp. She and Prem had eventually tied the knot as soon as he returned. Prem felt sorry that she wasn't able to join in the ministry, but he said she could come and help us with the deaf camps, and he even was willing to come sometimes if we needed a speaker.

We invited Bruce Schwalbe, a fine deaf American missionary from Bangalore, to be the speaker. Bruce was also a professor at the Baptist seminary and had a Christian deaf school in Bangalore.

All preparations were made. I was able to obtain a government holiday place for the handicapped for the camp in Poona, which was ideal. Several days before the camp, I had an unexpected telegram. It was from Rita, saying that she was unable to come because her mother-in-law was very ill. I was devastated, as I knew that I could not manage forty-five little deaf children for ten days

My girl Tara, who was married the day before the telegram came, was in her new husband Arvind's home city for receptions. Somehow, she got the message that Rita wasn't coming to help me in the camp. She was worried, she knew that I could never manage it on my own, so she shared this with her husband. He looked lovingly at her and said, "Tara, shall we cancel our honeymoon reservations in Goa and go to help your 'mom'?"

What a comfort it was when they arrived. We had invited forty-five children who could hardly read and write. Instead, to our surprise, ten deaf young people arrived. They of course, could already read and write. So, what we could not communicate with body language and the limited signs that I knew, we were able to write. It was so wonderful to see how quickly Tara and Arvind became one with these young people.

Tara was an art teacher and taught in one of our finest Christian schools in western India. She was able to take the art and craft classes and even picked up the signs and helped with the singing. Arvind had his master's degree in social welfare and was very competent in taking care of all the general administration, games and sports. He helped show videos and played the organ during the singing. We had a wonderful camp. The speaker was fantastic. He had brought flannelgraph stories and using pictures, the blackboard and especially lots of drama, he was able to share the message of the love of Jesus and salvation clearly. All those young people who had never heard of God or Jesus or anything about a personal relationship with God, accepted the Lord Jesus Christ and were saved!

But the most wonderful thing that happened was that during those ten days Arvind and Tara were confronted with the challenge of serving these precious deaf children and young people.

I was now approaching my sixty-sixth birthday and was facing a major decision in my life. The usual retirement age for our missionaries in Mukti was sixty-five. A year before I had handed in my resignation. My letter read, "Assured of the conviction that the ministry for which the Lord called me to Mukti has been fulfilled and that the national sisters and brothers are prepared to carry on the work of the Mission, I herewith request the Board of Governors to accept my resignation for work in the Pandita Ramabai Mukti Mission." To help prepare more Indian workers, I had been requested to stay on for one more year. I was glad for this, as it also gave me time to learn all I could about the deaf and to plan an upcoming deaf camp.

This had also given me time to contemplate what the future held. I knew it would be difficult to leave my Honeysuckle Family and the ministry that had become my life. My family and friends in Canada expected me to come home for they felt I had done my bit in India and I now deserved a more comfortable life at home. The mission was also months away from preparing national workers to take over the positions I held.

The predicament was that my heart had two homes. The question was, which one should I retire to?

Chapter Thirteen

My Second Call

The hours ticked away to the inevitable day of my retirement from Mukti—March 17, 1987—and the decision I knew I had to make. It was either to go back to Canada or stay in my beloved India, but with a new vision. I kept asking God to make it clear to me through His Word what I should do.

Common sense said that I should return to Vancouver and live out my remaining days on earth enjoying the beauty of that great city with my wonderful Mukti memories. A further pointer to returning to Canada was that my health was deteriorating at a fast pace.

Weeks of travel, tramping through the docks and customs' sheds at Bombay, running up and down stairs to meet officials and introduce them to Sheila Hamilton, an Indian co-worker whom I was training to take over the work of clearing goods through customs, was strenuous. Several shipments came at the same time. But I took it in my stride, until one evening, I suddenly told Sheila to hurry me to

Mrs. Dudha's—whose home in Bombay had become a home away from home for me—in a taxi. I had not been feeling too well, but had paid it no attention. Suddenly, there came a pain in my chest, as if a ton weight was resting on it, and I began to feel nauseous and my head was swimming and I was in a cold sweat.

I did not know how to sit or lie in the taxi. Mrs. Dudha called her doctor immediately. He said that I needed to have cardiograms, but I would have to wait until the next day because the clinic had now closed.

I rested at her home for three days and thought I was all right. I did tire easily and had occasional giddiness and perspired a lot, but I just thought a few days of rest would have me back to normal. However, my weight began to drop alarmingly and I lost ten pounds in a short time.

When I eventually returned to Mukti, I found that everyone was going to Dhond the next day as Prime Minister Rajiv Gandi was to be there. This was only fifteen miles from us and we realized it was a great opportunity for us to present our request for a postage stamp of Pandita Ramabai to be issued. I quickly typed up a letter for the superintendent to present, and got one of the blind little girls ready to present a basket made by the blind. Then Stutibala, our Honeysuckle baby was quickly dressed up in a sweet little dress. She was given a packet to hold tightly with Pandita Ramabai's *A Testimony* and our new annual report tied up with a flower that she was going to give to the prime minister when Mrs. Misal, the superintendent would present the letter.

There were nearly 200,000 people sitting in the field waiting to greet him. Security was so tight that no one was allowed within 100 feet of the helicopter pad and podium where he would speak. We tried to get the commissioner and other police officers to help us. They said they were sure that it would have pleased the prime minister to see the little ones, too, but no one was allowed to come near him, even to place a garland around his neck. We were told by the commissioner that if he allowed us, so many others would stampede to give garlands and requests. It was important to provide the needed security.

The prime minister arrived on the dot (not Indian standard time). We were seated right in front and the kids were thrilled to see the helicopter arrive before their eyes. The prime minister's speech was excellent (as much as I could understand the Hindi). In twenty minutes, he was finished and everyone rose to cheer and wave as he walked down from the podium—that is everyone but me.

I had been covering the little ones' heads with the end of my sari because the sun was so hot. I was feeling a bit uneasy and "heady," but got a shock when I could not get up from the ground. Vimalbai, Dorothy and Suprabha tried to hold me up, but I told them to watch so the kiddies did not get trampled underfoot. I tried to sit and hang onto the hot bars of the fence in front of us.

The police saw what was going on, and when they could not get our car near to pick me up, they immediately took me to the government ambulance still standing at the podium. I was rushed to the mission hospital as fast as it was possible through that crowd. They had no EKG unit there, but the government doctor had one in his ambulance. I was made to rest in the medical superintendent's office, and they brought the unit in. The doctors were concerned and ordered my immediate hospitalization and prescribed medication for me. I had been advised to have a stress test the week before in Puna, but could not get the report because I did not have enough money with me to pay the bill.

After the EKGs, x-rays and the other tests, I also went to the other hospital to see the cardiologist and to pay to get my stress test read. The doctor there, Dr. Mody, was so good. When he asked what I was doing, he tore up the bill and gave me a thorough examination and ordered an echocardiogram. Both the doctors who studied its results agreed that I had a slight heart attack, but that it was not as serious as had first been thought. I was hospitalized for five days and then had ten days of rest in a friend's apartment.

Still, it had been a warning to me. Then, on top of this, I had been trying to cope with excruciating pain in my hips and back. I'd had blood tests and x-rays and the doctors in Canada felt that the deterioration of my hip joints and my back problems were due in part to a thyroid problem that I'd had. To remove a thyroid growth in my neck, a Canadian doctor had given me an overdose of nuclear-activated iodine. It removed the growth, but it also caused a hypo or underactive thyroid condition that had then caused my hip and back pains. Even with strong painkillers, I could hardly walk. When the medication became in short supply, I was almost completely immobilized and confined to my room in Mukti. Only God's grace and an iron will helped me overcome the pain and enabled me to try to somehow keep to some kind of schedule of duties at the mission.

Then I had emergency surgery on my gallbladder. It was not looking good for me to stay in India. This latest setback, and other health problems that seem to hit all of us as our years advance, like a severe case of asthma that hospitalized me, were indicating that it might be necessary to "retreat" to Canada for retirement.

After my release from the hospital, I was then hit with a terrible attack of shingles (herpes zoster) all over the left side of my face, causing excruciating pain. I had to leave for a couple of months in Canada to get over this latest difficulty.

Yet despite all of these physical setbacks, and a very busy schedule on my return, my heart would not rest until God showed me clearly His call and the direction of His challenge to me. I praised God for return of health and strength and His guidance back to India. I knew He would show me further direction.

A Bolt Out of the Blue

But then some good news came, and it was like a bolt out of the blue from heaven. I was reading my Bible in my bed-sitting room just days before my formal retirement from Mukti. I was still anguishing over the decision that had to be made very soon, when it happened. The call to the deaf ministry was as clear as my first call to India in the first chapter of my life! Then it was contained in Isaiah 42:6 and now, in the very next chapter, God spoke to me again.

I had my Bible open and read on in Isaiah 43. As I waited upon the Lord, He led me to verses 8–19. Through my tears I read these portions, "Bring out the deaf who have ears but cannot hear. . . . You are my witnesses. . . . I will work and who will reverse it? . . . Behold I do a new thing" (KJV).

I had been aware that there was no Christian ministry to the deaf of any kind in our whole state of ninety million people. The Lord showed me His heart for the deaf and He gave me a heart that wanted to share that burden.

When the day of my retirement came at Mukti, it was no longer a sad occasion for me. For I realized that it was just the end of one chapter in my life and the start of another! After loving farewells and presentations at Mukti, as well as later in Canada, I officially retired in 1987 from the Publicity Department and my beloved Honeysuckle Family. I treasured the lovely gifts and plaques and speeches that were made by the school, the staff and my family. I knew that we would keep close, however far apart we were.

My years in the mission are a priceless treasure of miracles and happy memories, but I now had to prepare for the future, pain or not.

BIRTH OF A NEW MISSION

"Moushie," said Tara on the phone line to me at Mukti, before I packed up and left. "Arvind and I are coming to see you. We have something important to share with you."

"I can't wait," I said excitedly. "Come as soon as you can. I've got lots to tell you as well."

When this lovely couple came to see me, I felt my heart leap with joy as they shared with me their assurance of God's call to the deaf ministry and the good news that I could expect another grandchild—my twenty-ninth at that time.

They then showed me Isaiah 29:18, the verse that God had used to call them to this new outreach, "And in that day shall the deaf hear the words of the Lord."

Arvind went on, "Moushie, that day will be a reality because God has shown us clearly that we should join you in helping the deaf in this state to 'hear' for the first time of Jesus and His love and salvation."

The deaf in Poona were the first to hear at the camp we had held. But this was just the beginning!

I could hardly contain the excitement I felt. "Oh, that's so wonderful," I said as my voice trembled with joy. "This is an answer to my prayer. You see, God has also shown me through His Word that this is what I must commit the rest of my life to. I know that this will be the first spiritual ministry to the deaf in Maharashtra."

"Arvind," I said, "How could 900,000 deaf we have in our state have been so overlooked? The blind can at least hear the good news on Christian radio programs and in the churches, but how can the deaf hear unless we go to tell them? This will be a great ministry to these 'other sheep' whom the Heavenly Shepherd loves and whom He commands us to bring into His fold."

Arvind paused for a moment and then declared, "You know what, Moushi? I think we'll call this new venture, the Maharasha Ministry for the Deaf. What do you think?"

I nodded in agreement. A new ministry had been born just as a previous one for me had ended.

What a happy time we had in my room, sharing our hopes and plans for this new ministry. We agreed that, under God, we were a team!

A HOME IN POONA

After some discussion, we decided on Poona as the city where we would start the work. Located some 125 miles southeast of Bombay, it has a population of about one and a half million people, and is a gateway to the Bhor Ghat Pass, leading south to India's western coast.

We knew it would be very difficult to find a residence there, but God wonderfully provided a home for us to start the ministry in through Colonel Solomon (whom we called Uncle Solly) a Christian retired military gentleman. When he heard of my new mission, he readily made a house available for us to live in.

Arvind, Tara, their baby, and I, were able to move into a lovely, good-sized home where we could live comfortably and where the deaf could also come for meetings and social events.

Our next hurdle to climb over was to locate a place where we could base our work in Poona. It was almost impossible to find a suitable place that was easily accessible to the deaf by bus and that was suitable for a family to stay in. How we prayed and kept calling on the government offices trying to find a property in this huge and bustling city. The problem we faced was that the sites that were suggested were way outside of the city and difficult for the deaf to be able to reach by city transport.

When we heard that our state's chief minister was to pay an official visit to Poona, Arvind and I immediately dashed over to see if we could have an appointment with him.

"I am sorry, but you cannot make an appointment," an official at the government building told us when we arrived. "You will have to come back a little later when he arrives and wait in line to try to see him, just like everyone else."

My heart sank when I heard this, for I knew that with my hip and back problems I could not stand in line for hours. Yet I knew that I had to see this man to share our need. So I resorted to prayer and then dressed in my best sari. When Arvind and I returned that evening, we realized that we could be in for a long wait. It was a chaotic scene with hundreds of cars, scooters and bicycles parked all around the building and for blocks around it.

To add to our woes, when we got to the gate surrounding the building, we saw the line of people that appeared to be a mile long, all wanting to see the chief minister.

"What are we to do, Moushi?" asked Arvind.

"Just follow me to the office and let's see what the Lord will work out for us."

At the front desk, in my best Marathi I requested them to please consider giving me an appointment with the chief minister. "It is not possible for me to stand in line for hours because of my health," I explained, trying to catch my breath.

The man folded his arms across his chest, assuming a stiff, defensive posture. "I'm sorry, but you just have to go to the back of the queue," he said with an indifference that chilled me.

I felt a wave of anxiety wash over me as he spoke, and I shot up a telegram prayer to my Lord asking for His intervention in this impossible situation. Just then I noticed the three police officers who were standing beside us. One of them, his shoulders covered with brass stars, addressed me pleasantly in Marathi. Obviously surprised to see a foreigner speaking his language, he said, "Madam, I heard your request. It sounds urgent. Please follow me."

We were in a daze as the officer led us past the long row of people who had been waiting for hours, right up to the door of the room where the chief minister was meeting with the visitors. His personal assistant appeared to be standing at the door, so I bent very low and, in my best Marathi, asked him, "Could I please see the big Sahib?"

The man smiled and looked bemused at my request. It was then that Arvind whispered in my ear, "That's him! That's him!"

The chief minister asked me what I wanted, and I explained that I had come to present our application for land that was needed urgently to start our ministry for the deaf. He asked a few more questions about the work and then about the type of land we wanted. I then handed him my application and he looked at me as though he remembered me.

I was shocked when he then asked, "How are things going at Mukti?"

I began to search my memory for when we had met before. Then I realized that it had been when I was the guest hostess at Mutki Mission as well as the photographer and manager of the Publicity Department. I had met him when he visited the mission some years before.

"Things are fine at the mission," I finally was able to stammer out. "I have retired from there and now I am starting this new work for our state's deaf. They so desperately need our help at this time."

He again studied the application and then called out to his personal assistant, who was hovering close by, and told him to "attend to it immediately." As the man took the papers, the chief minister assured me that we would hear from him soon.

We thought it would be many months before we would hear anything, because these things move so slowly in India, but to our surprise, several weeks later we had an order giving us a property right in a convenient suburb of Poona. It was four acres of land on which would be built our Poona deaf center. On it we planned to have camps, conferences, workshops, accommodations for staff and a large administration building where rooms for training classes for the deaf in Bible, tailoring, computer, typing, carpentry, mechanics, electrical and horticulture could take place. It is difficult for the deaf to find employment unless they have training and a certificate.

The only requirement that the government had was that we plant 200 trees, which we would have done anyway.

How we thanked God for His gracious undertaking in supplying our need. Our application for registration of our ministry was accepted, but we had to change the name to Maharashtra Fellowship For Deaf.

HOW TO FIND THE DEAF

We now needed to find and reach the deaf in Poona. We started by visiting the deaf schools in the city and began weekly clubs for the deaf in two schools for several hours on Saturdays. These clubs proved a happy experience for children and young people. In the clubs we also helped them to develop skills through handicraft, art, music, signing, storytelling, audiovisuals, games and skits. We used gestures and body language to communicate.

We taught them Christian choruses and songs with signs, using bullock-cart bells, and we would tell Bible stories, but we were forbidden to use the name of Jesus Christ. It was interesting. When we told a Bible story and just mentioned God, some of the boys who had been at our camp would get all excited. They would wave their arms and get the attention of the others to let them know we meant the living God, Jesus Christ. We did not have to use the name of Jesus—they did!

From these clubs in several of the deaf schools, a Sunday School class developed in a Poona Methodist church. The young people wanted to know more about this God and brought in many other deaf every Sunday afternoon for several hours to the Sunday school that we started.

Every Sunday afternoon, we found our Sunday school room filled with enthusiastic deaf young people who were eager to "chat" with gestures and varied sounds which Arvind and Tara had picked up so well. After a word of prayer, it would be song time and how they loved it. Arvind would then use an overhead projector to throw the words to the wall of the crowded classroom. He pointed to them to help with the rhythm, and Tara stood beside him to lead the signing. She made them try to say the words as they gestured and made a "joyful noise" to the Lord while we provided the tune.

They loved the choruses and songs that had been translated into Marathi so that they could read them. Most of them had studied up to third or fourth grade at least, and all joined in lustily, sometimes wanting to repeat a chorus two or three times, as well as read the New Testaments given to us by a representative of the Gideons.

After a hearty song time, Arvind or Tara would tell a Bible story or lesson and then would use drama to teach lessons. Tara would also teach the deaf children simple Bible memory verses. We could never close the class in less than two hours, and even then they wanted to stay to chat about what they had "heard."

Arvind's and Tara's signs, body language and writing on the blackboard were instilling in them the biblical principles of trusting God for salvation, God's love and how to please Him through living a good life. It was wonderful to see how they responded to the Bible stories when they were performed in drama form. Some of the older young people who came to our house all the time were glad to help us prepare these dramas for the Sunday services.

It was marvelous to me how quickly Arvind and Tara, who both had master's degrees, were able to communicate with the deaf. As there was no sign language taught in my state, they would use gestures and body language which they picked up quickly. This meant a very limited vocabulary. What we could not demonstrate with our hands, we would write on the blackboard or dramatize.

All the deaf who came were young people, except Ramanlal, a middle-aged deaf man who did upholstery in cars in his family car business. He had heard from one of

Viola Dand with Boys from Pune Sunday School. Vahid (THIRD FROM RIGHT), from a Moslem family, was So Happy when He Received Jesus, Put the Cross on All His Works of Art. This was a Farewell Gift for Viola

the boys about our Sunday school and came with one of them. He would not miss a Sunday after that. It was so great to see him trying to sing the songs with enthusiasm and follow the message like the young people. He was so gracious and always willing to help with any repairs that we had or any upholstering that was needing to be done. Ramamlal was so appreciative of what we were doing for the deaf.

These Sunday school classes grew until there were over forty-five young people who came every Sunday. In fact, they would meet for almost an hour before we started on the steps of the church where they would be happily "conversing" with each other. Even though the Sunday school lasted several hours, the attendees were reluctant to leave when the classes were over.

Two of these boys who came from a family where their father was a member of the Shiv Sena, a political party with strong religious ties to Hinduism, which came into power in our state and defeated the Congress party that had always ruled Maharashtra State since the British hand-over in 1947.

When a deaf member of this political party heard of all of these deaf coming to our Sunday school, he first threatened some of the boys, and then one Sunday he appeared at the church.

"What are you boys doing in this Christian church? You are all Hindus!" he asked angrily. He pulled out a knife and threatened them. A scuffle ensued, but thankfully no one was hurt. But the janitor called the pastor.

The boys all fled. Several of the boys came back to tell us what happened and even dared to stay for a little while to hear the Bible story. The janitor and pastor, who had come out to see what happened and had witnessed the fight, decided to not allow us to use their room any more, because they did not want the church to get into legal problems.

It seemed as if our work might be ending just when it was growing so well. How were we to get over this problem?

Chapter Fourteen

ROCK OF AGES

I looked at Arvind and asked pointedly, "Aren't you going to visit these boys and assure them that we are here for them no matter what the opposition? They are welcome at any time."

Arvind smiled slightly. "Moushi, I will go and see some of the others that are leaders and find out what is happening. I saw them gathered in front of a store on the same street as the church is. I stopped and spoke to them and even though they are nervous after the threats, they long to be able to get together and are coming over here to us."

We were happy to see the boys come around cautiously and were encouraged to see how much they appreciated our support and encouragement.

The whole property for our deaf center in Poona looked like the *rock of ages*. In fact, when I first surveyed that rocky hillside land that we had been given, I couldn't believe that anything could grow there, let alone a deaf center be built on the site. The entire place was solid rock.

Arvind stood at my side and said, "Moushi, you look worried. Don't worry. It will happen. God has done one miracle in getting us the land, He will see that the deaf center that we need will indeed be a reality. I've already managed to find a work crew who will come to blast and level the property so we can get started."

Arvind then told me that the members of the Maharashtra Fellowship for the Deaf board, that had recently been formed, were coming for a dedication before they started blasting and leveling off the land, and before they could dig a well.

"Actually, they can't do anything until we have water," he concluded.

He had told me that government surveyors had been on the property to try to find a place where there was water so we could dig a well, but they found none. They had also been at the adjoining property, and had thought that the blind association that was planning a hospital for rural and poor blind there could find water on a certain spot, if they went down fifty feet. The well drillers had gone down 300 feet and still there was no water. It did not look very promising that we would be able to find water on our place. We reminded God of a promise in Isaiah 33:16, "Bread will be given him. His water will be sure."

We clung to this promise and planned for the well to be dug. One day I had a surprise visit at the house from our now-retired Pastor Hiwale from Kedgoan. He hobbled in supported by two canes, and said, "Salaam, Moushi. I heard that you needed water and were planning to dig a well on the property that God so wonderfully gave you through our state government.

"You will remember how God so wonderfully gave us water in the well we dug in Mukti when surveyors said we would not get any water in the area. I remember that you even stopped the studies in the school for three days to pray. You had the girls come before school in the mornings to lift out the rocks and dirt that the men had blasted the night before.

"Well, I have been praying for your ministry, and God has assured me that He will give you water on your rocky hillside. I have brought my little forked branch, so let's go and see what the Lord has in store for us." We bowed our heads for a word of prayer and then went out onto the street and flagged down a

Sharing the Rock Burden from the Mukti Well

motorized three-wheeler rickshaw and we were driven out to the site, about six kilometers away.

When Arvind saw the water-divining implement in the old pastor's hand, he voiced his opinion that he was not sure that this would work.

"Arvind," said the pastor gently, his old brown eyes locking on those of the younger man, "I know that God is going to show us the place where there is water."

School Girls Lifting Out the Rock Blasted for the Well in Mukti Mission

Arvind gently shook his head doubtfully, and when the pastor began walking on the property with the branched fork in his hand, he began to wonder what kind of magic this was. I followed behind with bated breath. The pastor stopped beside an anthill and said, "Let's pray. I think we may have found the spot." We bowed our heads and reminded God of His promise to us.

The pastor then lifted up the forked branch again and held it near the anthill. Suddenly, we saw it twist right over. I saw Arvind almost jump out of his skin. Then he asked if he could try. He held it over the same place, but nothing happened. Then, one of the other men took it, but he had no success either.

"Let me try," said Tara, taking hold of the stick. She stood by the anthill and the forked branch went over halfway.

The pastor looked at a little timer on his arm and said, "If you go down fifteen feet here you will find water."

I could see the doubt on Arvind's face. But Arvind said, "Well, let's pray and ask God to give us water as He promised."

Arvind then called in the men to blast and dig. Our wells in India are very wide and this one was going to be about twenty-five feet in diameter. Using dynamite, they blasted out the rock. They went down fifteen feet and sure enough there was a trickle. But, it was only a trickle.

Nanda and Dr. Sadgun, MFD President Beside our New Well

They went down another thirty-five feet of solid rock, blasting and lifting it out, and God answered our prayer. "His water shall be given" was the promise. Slowly the well filled up and has never been dry since. How we praised God!

Now the construction work could begin. Almost miraculously, Ziegfried Toews, a fine Christian architect in Vancouver, Canada, who had heard from the director of the Mennonite Central Committee that we needed helpers for our projects in India, made contact with me while I was home. He told me that he felt that God wanted him to do the architectural plan for that hillside deaf center.

So we met at his office and I gave him all the information I could about the site and showed him pictures. Not long after, he called me to come and pick up the beautiful architectural plans he had drawn up for the deaf center. He later became the vice president of our Canadian board for our ministry. His wife, Ruth, also works in his office and is a great support as she sees to our mailing list and other important messages and always provides the most delicious cakes and dainties for our board meeting coffee times. The architect, Zieg, shared his excitement over the project with the engineer, Len Hereema, who became the president of our board and has been a tremendous support to our ministry. He also works for the Canadian government and does engineering projects on the embassy grounds of the Canadian embassy in New Delhi several times a year. He usually flies down to Poona to see the work and to advise Arvind on technical matters.

How could we have dreamed of such wonderful help of people we had not even met before? But isn't it just like our great God who has promised, "I work and no man can turn it back" (Isaiah 43:13) and also "Behold, I will do a new thing. Now it shall spring forth" (Isaiah 43:19).

Now that we had water, the next step was to start construction of a pump house, storeroom, and an apartment for the security guard who was also the caretaker/janitor. He and his wife were living in a tiny, earthen-floor shack made of sheets of tin held down with stones. They could see the sunshine through the slits and the moon at night. But they never complained.

The security guard, Mahadik and his wife, Surekha, were the only Christians in their large Hindu family and had been coming to the Christian and Missionary Alliance church where Arvin and Tara were active members. They had been married for fifteen years and still had no children. We joined with them in prayer for a child. His Hindu father was after him to take another wife so he could have an offspring, but he refused. How amazed they were when God answered our prayers and they had a lovely son whom they called

Suhas (Great Joy) after over fifteen years of marriage! They are so grateful and he is a most conscientious worker on the grounds. There are other couples living in the building and they have built bathroom and toilet facilities for them and a tank to do their washing in.

THE COBRA SCARE

It was the monsoon rainy season. To catch the rainwater coming down the hill on the rocky site, a tank and retaining wall were being built out of the rock from the well. It was almost finished, and Tara and Arvind were at the site to help the workers complete it. I was at home working. Even though the sun had been shining moments before, suddenly there was a real cloudburst, which is common during the monsoon rains. I hoped Arvind and Tara had made it to the shed or they would be drenched. A little later they arrived and they were drenched! But, they were rejoicing, for in the five-minute downpour the tank had filled right up with water. We stopped for a word of praise and then Tara hurried to the bathroom to get out of her soaked clothes.

Then we heard a scream and the bang of the bathroom door. We ran to the bedroom and saw Tara's terrified face. There was a cobra in the bathroom! Arvind ran to the phone. A couple in their church were snake catchers. They had a snake house where they kept snakes they caught and sold them to the zoos and hospitals where they make medical treatment to cure snake bites of the venom. The couple arrived quickly, and the husband cautiously stepped into the bathroom with his rod and hook. He could not see the snake, but the drain in the corner had been left open for the soapsuds to run down after Tara had washed clothes on the bathroom floor. When he put the hook down the hole, he caught the snake. But it would only come up eighteen inches. The wife ran outside to the drain hole, opened the lid and saw that the snake had swallowed a frog in the drain and was stuck. She knocked the dead frog out of its mouth and her husband pulled it up.

He saw how frightened we were and decided he'd try to calm us down by entertaining us a bit. He quickly picked up the cobra by the tail and carried it to the living room and laid it on the couch. His wife handed him a piece of white paper. He began to crush it and tease the snake. The cobra immediately raised its hood, hissed and struck at the

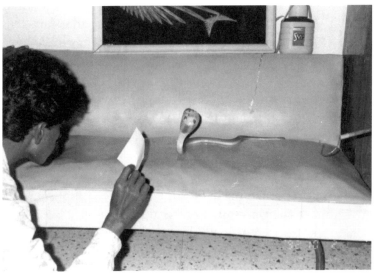

Teasing the Cobra on Living Room Couch

paper. After a few minutes of careful play (that didn't relax us as he expected), he grabbed it by the tail again and carefully put it in the bag his wife was holding and tied it up tight. Then they took off with it on their scooter. They told us they had to be careful, too, for that cobra had enough poison in it to kill at least a dozen people. We were sure this was true, for previously, a cobra got into our chicken coop, and we rushed out when we heard the noise of the chickens. Before we could get help to kill the snake, all ten chickens were dead. How grateful we were and thanked the Lord for protecting Tara and for the kind couple that saved our lives.

While the construction was going on at the rocky hillside, Arvind and Tara were also involved heavily with deaf fellowships which were being formed as a result of the deaf camps, which were well attended by deaf young people and deaf couples.

Bombay Blessings

Sunny and Seema Divekar, our staff workers in the Bombay deaf fellowship are seeing God do a wonderful work in the hearts of deaf young people and deaf couples in Bombay. The work has grown and a good group meet for up to five hours of happy fellowship every Saturday at the Bombay YMCA. Secretary P. P. Shinde arranged for them to have a recreation room for basketball, table tennis, etc. and a classroom for singing, Bible study, prayer and fellowship.

Every Saturday for four to five hours, with a snack in between, you'll find the happiest group of up to forty-five young people having a great time. They also have retreats and camps, both for young people and for deaf couples and

their children—special, blessed days several times a year. All are from Hindu families and several are Moslem, but how they love to sing and hear of Jesus and His love! It is such a joy to see the enthusiasm and outreach in witness of fine young people like Ajit

Ajit and Avinash after Bible Lesson with Questions and Seema Explains

and Avinash and many others who have accepted Jesus and who share their faith and truths that they discover in God's Word. They are ready to obey the Savior and want to be baptized and serve Him. Some face opposition and difficulties, but their trust is strong. A deaf Sunday school has also grown out of this fellowship and Seema meets with them since Sunny has to go to Nasik.

NASIK STATION EVANGELISM

The Deaf Fellowship was formed in Nasik, but with no other accommodation available to meet in, they decided to meet on the station platform if Sunny, our Bombay staff worker, would come and teach them. So, Sunny does the four-hour train trip every Sunday to Nasik. There he meets the young people on the platform who are so keen to learn of the Savior's love and they have a great time in signing songs, Bible stories and prayer, unhindered by curious crowds that stop to see the unusual sight of waving hands and odd sounds. Then they happily wave Sunny off on the train, signing "I love you" as he returns to Bombay. During the monsoon rainy season, if necessary, they move their Sunday School class, space permitting, to one of the waiting rooms which boosts the "congregation" who are intrigued with the enthusiasm of these deaf young people.

NAGPUR DEAF FELLOWSHIP

The Nagpur Deaf Fellowship meets regularly with Sanjay and Rekha Meshramkar, our volunteer workers there. Besides their regular fellowship meetings, the deaf young people gladly travel the twenty-four-hour train or bus trip to also attend our deaf camps held several times a year, and usually stay for another week or two with us for special Bible study after the camps.

Our work was blossoming. As part of a very effective outreach, we now have three or four camps a year in different cities around the state: Bombay, Nasik and other cities and holiday homes in the hills. The deaf came in good numbers which grew until we had up to seventy-five young people and deaf couples coming for the camps. It soon developed into the need to establish deaf fellowships in the five major cities of the state—Bombay, Nagpur, Nasik, Poona and in Aurangabad.

Our Bombay work has been particularly blessed. Sunny and Seema Divekar, our staff workers in Bombay, are seeing God do a wonderful work like the others, seeing precious deaf find refuge in the Rock of Ages.

PRAMILA'S NIGHTMARE

So many deaf are desperate with no one to help them. A very pretty deaf girl was brought to us. She weighed hardly sixty-five pounds and was in pain. Pramila, the pretty deaf girl, was only ten years old when her mother died. Her uncaring father deserted her. Relatives, not knowing what to do with her since she was deaf, sold her to scouts working for pimps from the red-light district in Bombay. She was trained to be a dancer to make money for them at nightclubs. She had a baby girl when she was twelve, but the baby's father (whom she lived with) sent her to the Gulf to make big money.

Several years later having contacted tuberculosis she was sent back to Bombay. Her "husband" treated her very cruelly, but a sympathetic guitarist fell in love with her and she became pregnant and had a baby boy. Her "husband" disappeared with their eight-year-old daughter and did not return. Unable to pay the rent, the landlord put her out on the street, sick, with her baby and baggage. There in the red-light area, a "client" recognized her and picked her up. Thinking that she and her baby would have a better chance outside of the area, he took her on the train and dumped her in a Poona suburb to fend for herself.

A lady passing by who has a home for beaten women saw the girl weeping and felt compassion for her. She gave her food and tried to help her find shelter. Finally, someone gave them our address and so they came to us with great hope.

Though we had no spare room, we could not turn her away. After several medical examinations, the doctors advised us to admit Pramila to the hospital. She was found to have an advanced case of TB and AIDS. We placed the baby boy in a Christian institution.

Arvind and Tara visited her, taking food, sharing the gospel and praying. Tara taught her crafts and Pramila made lovely things like a wall motto with Psalm 23:1–3 on it. Arvind brought her a Bible in her Telegu language. She was so excited! Pramila started reading it and responded to the gospel.

She made some recovery and was discharged from the hospital. Because Arvind and Tara were busy with deaf camps and Bible study sessions and I was in Canada for several months, Pramila went to stay with a friend in Bombay.

She returned several weeks later, looking very thin and ill. Out of loving gratitude, she brought lovely gifts she had made and bought for Arvind and Tara. She was admitted into the hospital again and doctors said it was just a matter of days—there was no hope. But, she had a great hope in Jesus and that there would not be pain, nor death, but eternal, glorious life awaiting her!

Desperately sick and vomiting blood, she never complained and tears of gratitude and joy often filled her eyes.

She had a great urge to go and see a dear friend who had been kind to her in Bombay. She was too weak to go and we tried to stop her, but she felt she had to go. We had no one to send with her. We never saw or heard from her again. She was so very weak that we wondered if she ever made it to Bombay or fainted and passed out in the train and was taken to a hospital near the station there and passed away.

We remembered how, with tears of gratitude and joy, she had said, "I'm ready to meet Jesus."

Chapter Fifteen

❧

THE DEAF SHALL HEAR

Eddy and Dolly were a deaf couple who attended our Sunday school in Poona. They had two young children and were a happy family who attended a Catholic church. Wanting to know more about our beliefs, they came to visit us in our home and we had the opportunity of sharing the way of salvation more fully with them.

During a subsequent visit one evening, they saw that we had a parcel with an interesting article about the "Wordless Book" lying on top of the box of books which had come from an organization called Wayfarers in the US, and they asked what this book was. I was able to share with them the message of the Wordless Book. It had five six-inch by six-inch colored pages of felt. I explained that the black page spoke about the sin in our hearts, the red page spoke of Jesus' blood that was shed to wash away our sins, so that our hearts would be white and clean like the white page. The green page spoke of growth which showed how, after our hearts have been cleansed, we could grow through God's Word in love and the ways of God. The yellow page spoke of heaven which would be our home if now our hearts were cleansed and we were ready to meet God.

"It is such a small, but wonderful book!" I told them. They nodded their heads with excitement. Dolly was fascinated and was ready right there to follow the directions of the little Wordless Book and give her heart to Jesus. Her husband, Eddy was enthralled, too, but did not make a public commitment like Dolly. Dolly saw another book there and it was a Bible.

"Would you like it?" I asked Dolly.

"Would it be possible?" she asked.

"Of course, it would," I smiled. With that I handed her the book that was full of the words of life—the Bible. How glad I was that it could be hers. I showed her how to read it, starting with the Gospel of John.

Dolly grew in her walk with God. One day when she came to visit us, she told us she was eager to serve God like we were. She asked if we could please give her typing lessons and maybe start a typing class for some of the deaf young people. In this way, she wanted to have a part in helping other deaf to know Jesus too.

Dolly came to us every day after she took her children to school, and we taught her typing. When we heard that she had a tailoring certificate and was teaching her trade to a couple of girls, we asked her if she could forget about the typing and could start a tailoring class for deaf girls.

We had been talking about and hoping to be able to start a tailoring class for deaf girls. She was happy about this, and the next week we had our first class. Six deaf teen-age girls came and they learned very quickly how to make patterns, practice their math on measurements and soon were ready to start sewing. We had only one sewing machine and were thrilled when several unexpected gifts of sewing machines were offered to us.

They would have a time of singing; how they loved the choruses and songs that Tara taught them. They signed and picked up the rhythm quickly. Then they enjoyed a Bible story and prayer before they started their tailoring lesson. This was a rewarding ministry for they would go home and share what they had learned with their parents. So the message went into many Hindu homes.

The girls did especially well in their exams and received their tailoring certificates. Jhoti especially excelled, so much so that the examiners were impressed. We asked her if she would be willing to come and teach a class, and the examiners felt she was capable. She was very happy about this, and now she is teaching a tailoring class with nine girls. Soon we will be having twenty deaf girls in two classes.

JHOTI'S EXAMPLE

The most exciting thing that happened was that Jhoti shared how she had accepted Christ. She did not have to tell us as she had become such a glowing, happy Christian and was a real example to the girls. Her Hindu mother was so impressed with what she had experienced that she wanted to know all about it. She took Jhoti's New Testament and started to read it. Then, every day, she would ask Jhoti what they had in the Bible class and they would have a great time going over it together.

When her mother came to visit us because she wanted to attend one of those Bible studies in the tailoring class, she told me how she had become interested in the message of the New Testament. We had the privilege of sharing with her more of how to know the Savior of that precious book. She is still studying the New Testament with great interest.

We now have two tailoring classes, one in Poona, and the other in Bombay. On the first floor of our staff quarters in Poona, is the tailoring classroom, two hostel rooms for the deaf girls who stay there, a kitchen, a guest room with bathroom, and a free area where the offices are housed temporarily until the administration building is ready.

We were so happy when we moved into our quiet hillside home on our rocky site. There were a school, and a few shops and buildings going up across the road.

Looking out of my bedroom window, I was fascinated with the work going on all over our property—all of it done manually. I watched the day workers breaking through the solid rock, pounding it into fine rock with big steel hammers. It would be carried away on the women's heads to the building site. The workers were all tribal people who were illiterate and who brought their children with them. They lived in little shacks that they had constructed out of straw, tin and stones that they had found on our site. Their children could not be in school, but this did not seem to bother them. My heart went out to them. I was anxious to start classes several hours a day so these children could learn to read and write, learn songs and hear stories of Jesus who loved them, too.

The construction of the administration building was also in progress. It was a large L-shaped building, with ten rooms on the first floor and several on the second. Classrooms were being built to train the deaf in the Bible, computer, typing, tailoring, electrical, carpentry, mechanical and horticulture skills. A Bible school course also was prepared for the classes which were soon to begin.

Nearly all the deaf who have since become our students are from Hindu homes. Many who have accepted Christ have shown their desire to be baptized. They are facing much opposition and even persecution. If they are put out of their homes when they are baptized, we hope that they can come to study the Bible and learn a trade here and stay in the dormitories that are nearing completion. We will also be able to have large camps on the site as the dormitories will be large enough to hold several hundred young people. There is a real need for the construction of the administration building and dormitories to be completed.

We have had difficulty in finding accommodation for the deaf who come to the camps from different places in the state. When the building work is finished here, we will have all of the camps here so that hundreds will be able to attend.

A chapel is also to be built and other residences for staff.

We face a large mandate. There are still over 900,000 deaf to be reached with the message of God's love and salvation in the Lord Jesus Christ. There is no other possibility of them getting the gospel. For ours is still the only spiritual ministry to the deaf in our state. We are determined that the deaf shall hear!

Chapter Sixteen

IN AURANGABAD, TOO

We were able to start a splendid school and hostel in Aurangabad for rejected and needy deaf girls. It was a miracle and came about through Mrs. Jyoti Kumar, a Christian attorney. She was the only daughter of the former commissioner of the city of Aurangabad, and lives with her husband and family in the United States. The father had come to Christ five years before his death and both Jyoti and her mother, who were dedicated Christians, wanted the big property on which they had lived, to go to some Christian ministry. They heard about the formation of our deaf ministry and contacted me and asked me to see them when they next came to India.

When we got word of her visit, Arvind and I went to meet Mrs. Kumar, and her widowed mother, who was still living there with her sister. We were very impressed with the two large bungalows on the one-and-a-half acre property that we knew would be ideal for the deaf hostel and school for which God had given us a burden.

We were happy to see the place and meet these dear people. The property was situated in an ideal part of the city with churches and colleges, a bus station, post office, hospitals and a power plant in the surrounding area. Everything was handy. There were two large bungalows: one was a beautiful eight-room home, which would be ideal for a hostel; the other had seven rooms, which had been used as a guest house for government visitors, and was rather dilapidated by then, but could be used for the deaf school. Even though these bungalows had become rather run down with no one living in them, we could see the great potential. It was a one-and-a-half acre property which would be ideal for camps and conferences. Although we could see that there were great possibilities, we knew that we were not in a position, at this stage in our ministry when there were so many other projects and urgent needs, to consider getting involved in procuring such an expensive property.

We also discovered that the many new companies that were coming into the city had offered big money for this valuable property since it was in such a prime location.

"You pray about it," said Mrs. Kumar, "and we will too. We know it will need a lot of renovation and painting. We would love to see a Christian ministry here in honor of our dear father and for the extension of God's kingdom."

She added, "Keep in touch and God bless you in your ministry."

And how we did pray! When she knew she was coming to India again, a couple of years later, she wrote several letters asking me to meet her again in Bombay and go to Aurangabad, for further talks about the future possibilities for the property. It was interesting that two days before going to meet Mrs. Kumar, I had seen in an American Christian paper, an advertisement by a coin collector. He had a list of valuable coins with a price for each. I remembered that I had a bag of coins that I had collected as souvenirs from different countries on my first boat trip to India. I managed to find the bag and discovered that American and other coins were in it, too. I had a coin of every one of the rare coins that were listed in the ad.

I had tried to phone long distance to find out if the coins that I had— which I totaled at $40,000 according to the ad—were really worth that much, but I could not get through to the man who had placed the ad.

In my Bible reading that night, I read how Moses was afraid to go to Pharaoh when God asked him to take the children of Israel out of Egypt to the promised land. He told God he was afraid to go because he did not think that Pharaoh would listen. God said to him, "Now go, and I will be with you." Then when Moses gave another excuse that he could not speak well and knew that Pharaoh would not listen, God said again, "Go now and Aaron will be your mouthpiece" (Exodus 3:16; 4:12).

It seemed that God was nudging me. We had prayed and now He was asking me to go ahead. So again, Arvind and I went to meet her in Bombay. When I shared with her about the Scriptures, Mrs. Kumar was impressed. When I told her about the coins, I wondered that if I managed to get the money for the coins, maybe we could consider renting the property on a long lease.

Mrs. Kumar phoned her husband in the US and spoke to him about this possibility. They were willing to let us have the property for a very reasonable rent, and the contract was made. We deeply appreciated this and were encouraged that our vision for the deaf girls could be fulfilled. I found later that the advertisement had been a fraud and my coins brought me only twenty-five dollars at a coin shop.

In a short time, the hostel was filled with girls. In a wonderful way, God called a matron, Mangala, whom I had trained in Mukti, who had been the matron of my Honeysuckle Family for a number of years before she was married.

Some teachers from a government deaf school there in Aurangabad had brought six deaf boys from their school to one of our camps. It was a wonderful camp and God did a great work in their hearts. Those teachers, although they were Hindus, and others, encouraged us to start a work for neglected deaf girls. There were many deaf girls, especially in the villages, who had no opportunity of having an education.

Delia, an ideal teacher, who has since been married to the son of a pastor across the alley from our hostel, felt called to join the ministry as she was a trained teacher for the deaf. She was placed in charge of the school where we now have more than thirty deaf girls. Some of these girls were rejected by their parents, many had been neglected and were from needy families. To see the wonderful transformation from such unhappy, needy girls into beautiful, happy, accomplished helpers, artists, clever students and good citizens is so rewarding. How they loved the Bible stories, songs and prayer times. They loved Jesus and tried to tell their families when they went home for school breaks; they tried to teach them to pray. Nearly all came from Hindu homes. It was a real faith venture. We had to provide all the food, clothes and bedding, as well as education, because most were from very needy homes. But how rewarding . . . and God is faithful!

ARCHANA'S STORY

Archana was seven years old when I first met her. Her parents and two brothers loved and cared for her until they discovered that she was deaf. They were so disappointed and she soon lost all worth and value to them. They left her to survive on her own while she still was a baby. As she was out playing alone among the bricks, she ate dirt and pieces of brick, for her father was a bricklayer. Her body became full of insects and bugs. As she got sicker they gave her no treatment, hoping she would die.

Neighbors saw how Archana was being neglected. They got after the parents and compelled them to take her to the hospital. The doctor scolded them for being so cruel and uncaring. Archana was given medicine to remove the worms and they came out like big piles of macaroni.

A relative of Archana's family had a girl, Sadhana, staying at our Aurangabad Hostel for Deaf Girls. They encouraged Archana's parents to send her there too. A year passed. Two of our staff members went for a visit. Mangala and Soniya went to the home and saw Archana carrying brick and sand for her father's work. Mangala scolded the father for sending the boys to school and using the little deaf daughter to do the hard brick work. He told her that the boys would study and then work, but what could a deaf girl do with an education? Mangala asked him to let Archana come to the hostel for a couple of days and see if she could learn. They were reluctant, and Mangala and Soniya had to leave.

Later, Archana's mother and a friend came to see the school. The mother was so surprised to see how happy the girls were eating lunch together, chatting with one another via sign language, clearing the table and even helping with the dishes!

Two weeks passed without word from Archana's parents. Finally, mother, father and a friend brought Archana. She did not cry when they left, for they had not shown her any love. She adjusted immediately. Now she is the cleverest, cleanest and one of the most beautiful girls in the school. She is very loving!

Several months later, when the parents came to visit her, her father cried when he had to leave. Mangala asked him, "Why are you crying? When she was so sick you did not care and showed her no love. Why are you crying now?"

He said, "It is as if she was dead because we cast her off. Now it's as though God has given us a new daughter—and we love her dearly. You have made her a new child."

It is truly the work of God and His love shown her that transformed this little girl. Archana prays so beautifully! She is always ready to ask the blessing at mealtimes. Her parents tell us that when she comes home for holidays, she tries to teach them to pray and be thankful to God. What a joy to see what God has done in this precious life. She is a joy to us all!

I remember how moved with happiness I was and how I gave praise to God when I saw the wonderful change in this sweet girl. How happy she was playing, singing, praying, helping and leading the smaller girls in games and other activities! How I pray that she will grow into a beautiful woman of God, helping others like her to know Him too.

Some of the girls have already completed the required four-year deaf curriculum in our school, and have their certificates and now are doing exceedingly well in tailoring classes in Poona.

We have two tailoring classes—in Poona and Bombay—one being taught by a deaf girl who has passed her tailoring classes with a certificate, and the other by a young deaf mother, Manda.

The next project was the staff quarters for our administrative staff. It was fascinating to see how that two-storey building, with a fine terrace on top, came up out of the solid rock that had been leveled off. We were reminded of the chorus, "The wise man built his house upon the rock."

Two levels of the ground floor houses the executive director Arvind and his wife, Tara, their two boys, Jacob and James, myself and Nanda, my handicapped girl. She has been a great help with the children and the cooking, cleaning and caring for the house. Tara is busy in the ministry teaching the deaf, managing the tailoring class and giving hospitality to visitors. We have a constant stream of visits in Poona of the deaf from other parts of the state.

We were happy Nanda could be with us. She had crawled into our hearts and home in the Honeysuckle Family—a little handicapped girl whose father gave her up when her mother died and the step-mother was not kind to her.

The girls were happy to have a sister whom they could help, but she surprised them by how much she could help them, too. She could even sweep the floor as she crawled on her hands and dragged her thin little legs after her. She loved school and did very well.

Nanda not only loved her new Honeysuckle Family immediately, but entered into everything as though she had always belonged. She was there only two weeks when I found her sitting on the floor in my room. She had a very sad look on her face. I was afraid that somebody had teased her. When I asked her, she said, "No. I have been listening to the stories and prayers in our prayer times together and the other girls say they know and love Jesus, but I know my heart isn't right and I would like to know Him and give Him my heart, too."

She had been reading my Bible the night before and was so sincere and knew what she was asking. My heart went out to her. How happy I was to lead her in the prayer asking Jesus to come into her heart, to forgive her sin and to make her His own child.

How she loved to hear the stories of the Bible. It was summer holidays at Mukti and all the girls were praying and asking God to help her to get a wheelchair before school started so she would not have to crawl to school. Every day she thanked Jesus for making her His child and she asked for the wheelchair, too.

Nowhere could we find the wheelchair, but we knew that God would answer prayer. Then a loving friend in Bombay asked someone she knew had one. That wheelchair had been given to an elderly relative, but she asked if she could donate the money to buy one for Nanda. What loving kindness! God had planted this in the heart of an Indian lady who had not even seen Nanda. That meant that we could order a wheelchair to be made. It would take six to eight weeks to complete it. By this time there was only one week left of the school vacation.

A few days later in Poona, a friend informed us that she saw a lovely, strong wheelchair that would be just right. Not only that, but an additional monetary gift was given by a loving friend because this one was more expensive. They had heard of Nanda and how she had given her life to Jesus. They sent the gift, praying that God's plan for her life would be fulfilled and that she would grow up to love and serve Him.

What excitement and joy when the wheelchair arrived at eleven o'clock the night before school opened. I placed the wheelchair beside Nanda's bed as she slept. If only you could have seen Nanda's excitement when she saw the wheelchair beside her bed in the morning and heard her sweet prayer of gratitude to her Savior who had answered prayer so wonderfully.

Nanda did well in school and I was able to help her get into a typing class and later into a computer class. This was possible because of a gift of a three-wheeler motor scooter on which she could go back and forth, donated by the Poona Rotary Club.

Nanda had come to stay with us in Poona. She was able to go to the classes on her own, even in the heavy traffic. She did well and also took a secretarial and a telephone operator's course and got a job. When the heavy monsoon rains came, she was unable to go to work on the crowded, muddy roads. We were happy because we needed help at home. Nanda then took on the responsibilities in the home. She became a great helper with the cooking, housework and with my two "grandsons" (Tara and Arvind's sons). I have over fifty grandchildren, by the way, who are the sons and daughters of my Honeysuckle girls who were married.

Nanda has been such a loving, helpful part of our family. Just recently, there was a great need for an efficient staff worker in the Aurangabad hostel. She prayed about it, and felt she would like to become an official staff worker and go to help out with the need there. There are nearly thirty girls in the hostel and she has become a happy part of the staff there, loving the girls and helping the staff in their care and training.

THROUGH THE FIRE

What happened to Beena Shrisunder's life is shocking beyond words, but so is the miracle that has happened to her. Beena's father was married three times. He became a total alcoholic and his wife soon became overwrought from his abuse. When she could take it no longer, she took a tin of kerosene, poured it over herself, lit a match and set herself on fire.

After her death, the husband repented and asked her father for his wife's sister, promising to make up for what he had done to the sister. For a while all went well. Then he became addicted to alcohol again and was worse than he had ever been. They had a lovely little daughter, whom they named Beena, born on November 17, 1985. The abuse had become so unbearable that Beena's mother, absolutely distraught, followed her sister's example. She asked Beena to get the kerosene can, poured it on herself and right in front of her seven-year-old daughter, went up in a blaze.

This was such a terrible shock to Beena that on the spot she lost both her hearing and her speech. The father could not manage her alone, so he married a third wife. The stepmother soon became unhappy with the alcoholic father. In her anger, she took it out on the deaf daughter, whom she could not stand, either. She was not given food on time and was completely neglected. The emotional trauma caused Beena to withdraw completely; it was almost impossible to communicate with her at all. Her great need for love showed only when she played with the dog. No one paid attention to her or thought of her future.

After some time, Beena's grandmother realized her condition and went to see a social worker, from whom she heard about our hostel. She was given our address and brought Beena to us. At first we wondered how we could take her in, because we could see what a very sad effect her past had had on her. But when we heard her story, we were moved and longed to be able to help her. We realized how much she needed love, and accepted the challenge.

How difficult it was at first to see no response, but once she realized that she was dearly loved, she began to mix with us. Smiling and muttering to herself slowly increased, and she began to respond to the love shown to her. God proved He could give victory when one loves with all the heart. The change in her and her happiness is a miracle.

Her hugs mean almost more than any others. She always smiles as she signs and makes sure we see her sign of "I love you." She is doing well in school, signs as she smiles, sings and prays.

Chapter Seventeen

India's
Cornerstones

Looking back on my forty-six years in India, and recalling all the miracles that have happened, it has been so rewarding to see how the *light* has shone into so many hearts in that land of darkness. It is almost overwhelming!

Could anything in the world be more wonderful or worthwhile than watching these dear girls in the Mukti Mission—the Home of Salvation—and the precious deaf in Maharashtra, come to life through the Light of the World, our precious Savior?

I think of what a joy was mine to care for and train my Honeysuckle Family of thirty-four girls, as well as to serve the Lord in the school, in the Publicity Department and many other blessed ministries. The words of Psalm144:12 come back again and again to me: "That our sons may be as plants grown up in their youth; that our daughters may be as cornerstones, polished after the similitude of a palace."

In the deaf ministry, too, we have seen God's wonderful care and love for these precious people. It has been more than rewarding to have a share in their lives. Already in the ten years during which we have ministered to the deaf, we have witnessed lovely young people, now trained and dedicated to God, become ready to be His cornerstones. We look forward to seeing many of these go to the Bible school which we are hoping to open very shortly. The course has already been prepared, that they may become the cornerstones—evangelists, pastors, and trained workers—to reach out to the over 900,000 deaf in our state alone who still need to know of salvation and the Savior's love for them.

My goal is to see at least three deaf churches planted in our state by the year 2000.

The Heavenly Father knows and sees so well that the time is coming when the Christians in India may have to stand alone. It is with joy we see God preparing cornerstones in India. They need us so desperately as they face opposition, and even persecution, for following and obeying Christ.

When I saw in Indian newspapers the demand by orthodox Hindu organizations that foreign missionaries should "quit India immediately," I realized that it could be that the time of Western missionaries in India could be soon be over. This has made the task of training national workers even more challenging and essential. For it is they who can continue the caring ministry of helping others and evangelizing in these days.

May these girls who have grown up in Mukti, and many more in the deaf ministry, who have been saved by the Heavenly Shepherd, present a challenge to us all.

In Zechariah 10:8, we read: " . . . they shall increase as they have increased."

God can only increase them through you and me, His Church, for there are still so many to be reached. Of the population of over 900 million in India, only two-and-a-half percent are Christians.

Other handicapped, like the blind and lame, are able to attend church and hear the gospel. They can also hear it on radio programs and the occasional Christian television programs that are broadcasted in India. But what about the deaf? There is no way that they can know the gospel unless we, and those who have found the Savior, the Light of the world, reach out personally to them and present the message in a way they can understand.

Of the 90 million population in my state of Maharashtra alone, there are over 900,000 registered deaf, as well as thousands more who live in the slums and villages. May we not fail God who has so graciously become our light and salvation. May we through intercession and with the support of those who have been enlightened in India, and are seeking to make Him known, do our part. "He died for all, that those who live should no longer live for themselves, but for him who died for them, and was raised again" (2 Corinthians 5:15).

May I challenge you to have a part in the rewards of intercession and sharing with us to be His torchbearers of the *light to India*!

Epilogue

The Rest of the Story

L ike many who have heard my story, you may wonder, "Whatever happened to Lloyd?" Let me tell you the rest of the story.

I was not sure how I would be able to face Lloyd when I next met up with him. The opportunity came during my first furlough back in Canada. I was on my way by train on November 22, 1963, to the Toronto area as part of a deputation speaking tour, when I was shocked to hear the news that that the US President, John F. Kennedy, had been assassinated in Dallas, Texas.

I was to stay in the home of a Baptist pastor and his family. After I was brought there from the station, we all sat stunned in the living room of their home, our eyes glued to the television as continual updates on this terrible event that was reverberating around the world were being given.

The phone rang and the pastor answered it. Vaguely, in the background, I heard him saying, "Yes, yes," but I paid it no attention, as the J. F. K. murder was claiming all of my attention.

As he sat down, the pastor said casually, "Lil, it was Lloyd James."

As I heard this, I felt my face flush. It was then that I remembered that Lloyd had been an usher in this pastor's church at the time we had ended our relationship.

As if reading my mind, the pastor said, "He's living in the suburbs now. He said he had read in the *Toronto Star* of your meetings in the area and knew that you would be speaking here in church tomorrow night."

I sat there mute as he added, "Lloyd wants you to know that he is coming with his wife and wants you to stay with them overnight. He will see you off at the train station on Monday morning as you go back to Vancouver. He's going to take some time off from his job at the Bell Telephone Company."

All I could do was mutter, "Oh, no, how can he do that?"

"Don't worry, Lil, it's not a problem for him to get some time off work."

But *that* was not my problem. I wondered how I could face him again.

When the service began on the following evening, I allowed my eyes to search the congregation from my vantage point on the platform, to see if I could spot Lloyd and his wife, but there was still no sign of them.

Soon it was time for me to speak about the work in Mukti. I was partly through my message when I spotted Lloyd sitting alone in his seat halfway back, beaming as he listened intently to my story. I had thought that I would forget what I was supposed to say if I did see him, but instead it inspired me to see him so interested, and that made me want to share even more articulately.

Once the service was over, that initial nervousness came back as a crowd began to form around me with questions. There were reporters from the local press, people from the church who wanted to chat with me about India, and Lloyd!

After a few minutes, the group thinned out to Lloyd and me and it was now time to talk face-to-face. We did not need to say anything. He smiled and told me that he had been inspired by my presentation.

As we walked out to his car, Lloyd put his hand on my shoulder and said, "Lil, I have two lovely girls, they can't wait to see Dad's old girlfriend!" I smiled, and from then on, we chatted just like good friends. When we arrived at his home, I met Grace, his lovely wife. We had a beautiful time just talking together. There was no embarrassment, but mutual Christian love.

That was the beginning of them getting behind my ministry. We kept in touch through the prayer newsletters that I sent out.

When I returned to Toronto on another furlough, I received a message from the two of them saying that they knew that I would be in the Toronto area again and wanted me to come and stay with them in their home during my week there.

It was a great week with both Grace and Lloyd, who were enthusiastic to help me with the literature table for the ministry. Each evening Lloyd would operate the slide projector so I could speak from the platform. Lloyd saw how tired I was from the travel and constant meetings.

During one meeting, when I had to answer questions from the audience, I was asked about my "call" to the mission field. I had to be very tactful in how I explained it, but I did briefly mention how I had given up marriage to obey God.

When I saw Grace shedding some tears, I felt badly about what I had said. Later, I apologized to her. It was then that she told me her story. "Lillian," she said, "I thoroughly understood and I thank God for the way He has led me, too. You know, I also had been engaged to a Canadian airman like Lloyd. Two months before our wedding, he was shot down over London." I was stunned and felt a real love towards Grace and was so pleased that she had become Lloyd's wife.

Our friendship blossomed from there on. They continued to share in my ministry through prayer and also with gifts for my Publicity Department. Our fellowship was blessed. Several years ago, I had a letter from Grace saying that she wanted me to know immediately that, two days before, Lloyd had had a massive heart attack and that he was now "in Glory."

My furloughs were always full of many interesting and exciting adventures. I traveled not only in Canada and the US, but I also had meetings in New Zealand, Australia, Europe, Great Britain and even traveled to Athens, Greece, Hong Kong and Jerusalem.

I am grateful to God for the many friends who have so faithfully stood with me in prayer and support. They too shared in the call to be a light for God in India. Many have come to visit our work there. I am also grateful for the faithfulness and help of Viola Dand, who came to Mukti on several occasions and, on her last visit, stayed four months to help Arvind set up a filing system for our deaf ministry. Also, for Signe Oliver, Eleanor Tate, the Wally Klassens, Vidyul who had been our much-loved Honeysuckle baby, Audrey Beckett and others who have visited and so faithfully support me and the ministry.

I would like to express my appreciation for the loving fellowship and work of the councils of the Ramambai Mukti Mission and also the Mahahrashtra Fellowship for the Deaf. How I thank Dr. Ed Kemprud, who was our first president and who started the American council. Ed has been a great supporter to me personally and to the ministry. His niece, Cindy Payton, who is secretary and her husband, George, who is now the US president of our board, are doing a tremendous work in our deaf ministry.

I have experienced a number of severe health problems and I am no longer able to cope with the hot season in India. So I spend six months every year in Canada for medical reasons and then six months in India. I am so grateful to Anjali, one of my Honeysuckle girls, who became a flight attendant with a major airline and gets all my tickets for me, so I can come back to Canada for medical purposes. She is the first girl from the thousands in Mukti to work in this way for an airline, and is so glad she can help God's work and the ministry in this way. How wonderfully God works.

I am still spending that amount of time each year in India to share in the needs of the ministry there. I cannot get away from the challenge of reaching and training the deaf to come to know Christ and then to become the future leaders for Him that are so urgently needed. I trust Him to let my goals become a reality.

He called me to be "a light to the nations." May those who have come to the light in India, pierce the darkness in a new and powerful way with God's message and truth.

ABOUT THE AUTHORS

LILLIAN DOERKSEN is a true missionary hero. This Canadian-born woman, who many have likened to a Protestant Mother Teresa, has spent forty-six years of her life caring for the children of India, first of all with the Pandita Ramabai Mukti Mission in Kedgoan, Mahahrastra State, where she helped "mother" thirty-four girls, whom she calls her "Honeysuckle Family." She retired on March 17, 1987, from the Mukti Mission—the Home of Salvation—and at the age of 66, should really have left India because of her declining health.

But then Lillian received a second call from the Lord, this time to work with the 900,000 deaf in her state. Instead of returning home to Vancouver, British Columbia, to live out her retirement, she founded the Mahahrashtra Fellowship for the Deaf. This pioneering and inspiring work provides spiritual help and vocational training to deaf young people, girls and couples who otherwise would be ignored by their society.

Lillian Doerksen has truly provided *a light to India*!

Dan Wooding is an award-winning author, journalist and broadcaster who was born of British missionary parents in Nigeria, West Africa. He now lives in Southern California with his wife, Norma, where they founded and run a Christian non-project outreach called ASSIST (Aid to Special Saints in Strategic Times). Wooding, who has authored or co-authored some thirty-four books, is also a commentator on the UPI Radio Network in Washington, DC, and a syndicated columnist for publications around the world.

To order additional copies of:

A Light To India

send $16.95 plus $4.95 shipping and handling to:

WinePress Publishing
P.O. Box 1406
Mukilteo, WA 98275

or have your credit card ready and call:

(800) 917-BOOK